IS NOTHING SACRED?

IS NOTHING SACRED?

The Non-Realist Philosophy of Religion

SELECTED ESSAYS

Don Cupitt

Fordham University Press
New York
2002

Perspectives in Continental Philosophy No. 28
ISSN 1089–3938

Library of Congress Cataloging-in-Publication Data

Cupitt, Don.
    Is nothing sacred? : the non-realist philosophy of religion : selected essays / Don Cupitt.— 1st ed.
        p.   cm. — (Perspectives in continental philosophy ; no. 28)
    Includes bibliographical references and index.
    ISBN 0-8232-2203-9 (hardcover)
    1. Philosphical theology. 2. Subjectivity—Religious aspects—Christianity. I. Title. II. Series.
    BT40 .C79   2002
    210—dc21   2002003059

Printed in the United States of America
02   03   04   05   06   5   4   3   2   1
First Edition

CONTENTS

ACKNOWLEDGMENTS

I thank the various publishers and editors who have permitted me to reprint those pieces in this volume that have already been published elsewhere. They are as follows:

"Kant and Negative Theology" (chapter 1) was contributed to the Donald MacKinnon *Festschrift*, Brian Hebblethwaite and Stewart Sutherland, eds., *The Philosophical Frontiers of Christian Theology* (Cambridge: Cambridge University Press, 1982). Chapter 2, "Faith Alone," first appeared in Peter Eaton, ed., *The Trial of Faith* (Worthing, England: Churchman Publishing, 1988). Chapter 3, "Anti-Realist Faith," first appeared in Joseph Runzo, ed., *Is God Real?* (London and New York: Macmillan, 1993). Chapter 4, "Free Christianity," was written for Colin Crowder, ed., *God and Reality: Essays on Christian Non-Realism* (London and New York: Mowbray/Cassell, 1997).

Chapter 5, "Is Anything Sacred?" was published in the journal *Religious Humanism*, then edited by Mason Olds, Vol. XXIV, Number 4 (Autumn 1990). Chapter 6, "The Human Condition: Diagnosis and Therapy," was first published in *Resurgence* magazine, Satish Kumar, ed. (March/April 1993), and then subsequently reprinted in *Only Connect: Soil, Soul and Society*, John Lane and Maya Kumar Mitchell, eds. (Totnes, Devon: Green Books, 2000). Chapter 8, "The Radical Christian World-View," appears in the 50th Anniversary issue of *Cross Currents*, Vol. 50, nos. 1–2 (La Rochelle, N.Y.: Spring/Summer 2000). This journal is published by the Association for Religion and Intellectual Life (ARIL).

Chapter 9, "The Value of Life," appeared in *The Modern Churchman* NS, Vol. 32, No. 2 (1990); and chapter 10, "Nature and Culture," was published in Neil Spurway, ed., *Humanity*,

Environment and God (Oxford, and Cambridge, Mass.: Blackwell, 1993).

Finally, chapter 11, "Reply to Rowan Williams," appeared in the journal *Modern Theology*, Vol. 1, No. 1 (October 1984); and the "Reply to David Edwards," chapter 12, was written at his invitation and published in his *Tradition and Truth: The Challenge of England's Radical Theologians, 1962–1989* (London: Hodder and Stoughton, 1989).

A number of the pieces have been a little revised for this volume.

D. C.

INTRODUCTION

What, you may well ask, is an English philosophical theologian doing in a series of books about Continental philosophy? Under all normal circumstances it is understood to be the duty of English academics to shelter the minds of the young from noxious Continental ideas; a duty which, until recently, all English philosophers and theologians performed unhesitatingly and with great success. When I first became a Fellow of a Cambridge college in 1965, I found that the college library, though very large, still contained not a word of either Freud or Marx—and indeed almost nothing of any other Continental thinker since Kant, either. In those days the Channel was wider than the Atlantic.

Today, things are very different, but many senior people do not approve. Thus Mary Warnock (Baroness Warnock), a much-loved and respected member of the postwar Oxford generation of philosophers, expresses her distaste by bracketing Derrida, Rorty, and Cupitt together as enemies of objective truth and public morals.[1] Now, *that's* the sort of criticism that really cheers me up—and it helps to explain how I come to be figuring in this series of books.

How did I get to be so Continental? It is true that English thought has usually sought to protect established institutions; but I was made aware of serious internal conflict *within* the Establishment culture at an early age. At my school, I was presented with, and deeply influenced by, two distinct systems of thought. One was Darwinism, with which I fell in love as soon as I understood it; and the other was the Christian Platonism of the old Anglican high culture. When I reached

---

[1] Mary Warnock, *An Intelligent Person's Guide to Ethics* (London: Duckworth, 1998), pp. 116ff.

the Sixth Form I became head of my House and a school Monitor, which admitted me to the school's inmost privilege—a weekly hour for the dozen or so of us most senior boys in the Headmaster's study, reading Plato's *Republic* aloud with him. It was all very Victorian: we were being taught the ideology of an Imperial ruling class and we were learning its ethic of service. To us much had been given, and of us much would be required.

By the age of 17, then, I had been deeply impressed by both Darwinism and Platonism. I have loved big systems of thought ever since: but how was one to deal with the obvious conflict between these two?

At 18 I went on to Cambridge, and there began by studying Natural Sciences, including in my second year an optional course in a subject then rather new: the history and philosophy of science. I was introduced to the decidedly unplatonic ideas that truth has a history and a social setting, and I first considered the possibility of a pragmatist, rather than a realist, philosophy of science. Newtonian gravity, for example, seemed to be realistically unimaginable: what could this "force" be that seemed to act at a distance and to be unaffected by any interposed material? Might it not be simpler to treat the so-called "force of gravity" as being merely a rule for doing sums that has been found to work well? At this time, my philosophy of science teacher, the late Russ Hanson, also introduced me to Wittgenstein, in the very year that *Philosophical Investigations* was published. The famous duck/rabbit drawing was used to teach me that in perception we do not just passively register our experience: we put a construction upon it. Interestingly, we need what the psychologists call an "object hypothesis" in order to help ourselves to see more clearly. Perception is from the first interpretative—a new idea in those days, but nowadays commonplace. In my own early writings, I already refer to what I call "the interpretative plasticity of the world": several *different* interpretative frameworks can be imposed upon the world, and can seem to be confirmed by experience.

In October 1954, I began to study theology with a view

to ordination, and naturally opted to include a course on the philosophy of religion. Of the British, I liked David Hume most, and studied him the most thoroughly. Reading his famous pages about causal necessity, I was struck by the line: "the mind has a great propensity to spread itself on external objects,"[2] which seemed interestingly to blur the traditional sharp distinction between the inner and outer worlds. I liked the implied constructivism of Hume's account.

At that time, and while preparing for ordination, I reckoned myself a pretty traditional Christian. Since the early nineteenth century, "low church" Anglicans had looked to Pietism and the Evangelical Revival, and "high church" Anglicans looked to Rome and to Thomas Aquinas. I was of the latter party. I was still a metaphysical theist, but I disliked any kind of anthropomorphic or interventionist language about God. I pursued the Negative Theology, and identified with the character who is called "Demea" in Hume's *Dialogues Concerning Natural Religion*.

During my student years, however, I also began to meet and to be impressed by the most important intellectual tradition in modern religious thought—and the one that many Anglicans tend to neglect—the great Lutherans, and in particular Kant, Kierkegaard and Bultmann, whose influence over me slowly grew and deepened over twenty years. Kant, after demolishing the traditional "proofs" of God's existence, had put forward a non-realistic idea of God as a regulative ideal of reason, and had suggested how images of God might best be understood as functioning to guide our attitudes and our moral conduct. The others—Kierkegaard and Bultmann—were in those days classified, along with many other modern Continental thinkers, as "existentialists;" a dead label today, but at least it encouraged one to read religious doctrines not for their "speculative" or metaphysical content, but for the way they might be appropriated and enacted in one's own life. Thus one might say, for example, that to believe in the doctrine of

---

[2] David Hume, *Treatise*, Bk. 1, Part 3, Sect. 14 (Selby-Bigge edition, p. 167).

the Creation of the world out of nothing is not a matter of holding to a certain theory in speculative cosmology, but rather a matter of continually receiving one's own life as a pure gift, and living it out accordingly.

I now have just one more source of the non-realist philosophy of religion to mention. It derives from the British debates of the 1950s and 1960s about the verification principle. The controversies were complicated, but the common thread running through them was a challenge to believers: "If you want to claim, as you surely must, that your beliefs are in some way factually, or empirically, or objectively *true*, then you must show in detail just how experience can confirm their truth, and just what events and experiences might oblige you to give them up, or at least drastically to modify them." The orthodox, or those usually reckoned orthodox, accepted the challenge and tried to explain how throughout our lives, faith is permanently on trial, as some events seem to confirm it and others to tell against it; but (said the orthodox) we also believe in a final vindication of faith after our deaths, and the whole of our theology is a spelling-out of that hope and of the reasons why we adhere to it. So much for the orthodox: but there were also those who rejected outright the view that faith makes quasi-factual and empirically-testable claims.[3] R. M. Hare saw faith as a way of committing oneself to certain cosmic attitudes, such as patience and hope in the face of adversity, or cosmic thankfulness when things are going well for us. R. B. Braithwaite saw a profession of faith as expressing an intention to live according to Christian moral principles, as they are illustrated in the body of Christian stories. And thirdly, from 1965, the young D. Z. Phillips began to put forward his own Wittgensteinian approach to the philosophy of religion: we should not make the mistake of supposing that religious beliefs are like scientific theories, and can be tested in a similar

---

[3] For the writers discussed below, see Anthony Flew and Alasdair Macintyre, *New Essays in Philosophical Theology*, vol. 4 (London: SCM Press, 1955); R. B. Braithwaite, *Theory of Games . . . and An Empiricist's View of the Nature of Religious Belief* (1955; reprinted Bristol: Thoemmes Press, 1994); and D. Z. Phillips, *The Concept of Prayer* (London: Routledge, 1965).

way. We should limit ourselves to showing what religious language is, and how it works. When we have done this in full, there is no more to say: either one finds oneself wishing to join in this form of life and play this game, or one prefers not to do so.

We now see that all the elements of the non-realist philosophy of religion were around by the mid-1960s in Britain. They included the old Negative Theology, the philosophy of Kant, the existentialist theology, with its emphasis upon the life of faith as an appropriation-process (one appropriates doctrines to oneself and enacts them in life), the various new "noncognitive" philosophies of religion, and the pervasive multiculturalist thought of the interpretative plasticity of the world. *We* are the world-builders, and different peoples build different worlds. Religion and morality are cultural and historically evolved, and all gods are tied to the peoples who have posited them.

In the 1970s I picked up a further idea from early eighteenth-century theology, where one sometimes finds writers distinguishing between the "absolute" and the "relative" meanings of the word "God." The absolute or metaphysical use of the word God refers to God as an infinite spiritual substance, self-existent Being, the world-cause, objective and distinct from us. The relative use of the word "God" refers to a person's (lower-case) "god" as that which has highest authority in his life. It is what Tillich called his "ultimate concern." It is what he lives by. It is not a being, but his ideal, his dream, his hope, his ambition, his calling, his task, and his guiding star, that to which his whole life is oriented. Following St. Paul (Philippians 3:19) a preacher may say scornfully that there are people "whose god is the belly;" but to my eighteenth-century predecessor at Cambridge, Edmund Law, "there is only one Eternal Self-existent Being which bears the Relation of God to us."[4] To Law it is obvious that the existence of the metaphysical God can be proved, and he reckons he can show

---

[4] Edmund Law, trans., *An Essay on the Origin of Evil, by Dr William King. Translated from the Latin, with large Notes*, 3rd ed. (Cambridge 1739), p. 80.

that God absolutely is and must be our only (relative) god. O God, be my only god! But suppose that we become acutely aware of our own human limits: we realize that we are always inside our human language, and only ever see the world through our human eyes. All that is ever accessible to us is the relative god, my god. As I see this, metaphysics dies and I am left knowing only my god, my guiding religious ideal. And that is the non-realist philosophy of religion in a nutshell.

It sounds at first very simple: Christian belief *minus* its traditional objective or metaphysical content *equals* Christian non-realism. Only the subjective side of faith is kept—but it is the side that counts most. This is Protestantism squared: the old Lutheran and existentialist demand for the thoroughgoing appropriation of faith into oneself and its enactment in one's living, now taken to its logical conclusion. As Albert Schweitzer used to claim on behalf of his own version of these ideas, they represent a thorough purification and spiritualization of Christian belief. I could envision a non-realist systematic theology: God is the religious ideal, and Christ the embodiment of that ideal in a human life. I believe in Christ's Resurrection just insofar as I am living a new and risen life inspired by him. Christ's Ascension is simply his becoming the Lord of those who look to him. To believe in Providence is to believe that our faith, if we stick to it, will always pull us through.[5] Intercessory prayer is a communal way of expressing love and giving support. Non-realism seemed to offer a new and better interpretation of every line of the Creed.

It is not as easy as that. I soon found that the shift to the non-realist point of view was very hard to explain. A very few people could see at once that it was the next, inevitable step after the debates of the 1960s; but most people were and are uncomprehending and outraged. Academics and church peo-

---

[5] The classic statement of this theme was given by Tillich in a sermon on the meaning of Providence in *The Shaking of the Foundations*. Notice that many of the attributes of God—his might, his being a refuge, his power to console, and so on—are nowadays regularly transferred to human *faith*, an interesting demonstration that many more people are non-realists than are ready to admit it publicly.

ple were just as angered and affronted by *theological* non-real-ism, as members of the scientific establishment are by *scientific* non-realism. The reason in both cases is doubtless the same: any great Establishment that controls a large body of truth, defending an orthodoxy and the interests of a great profession, seems politically bound to take a dogmatic-realist view of the status of the body of knowledge that it guards.

Not only was I in dire trouble with the Establishment, both academic and ecclesiastical—the two in England being, still to this day, surprisingly interwoven—but also the changeover to the non-realist point of view soon turned out to have very much more difficult and wide-ranging repercussions, both in philosophy and in theology, than I had expected. In retro-spect, I see that I was belatedly learning something that both Marx and Nietzsche knew perfectly well: the critique of reli-gion, when it is completed, provides the basis for the critique of everything else; the Death of God—the old metaphysical God, that is—doesn't leave the world otherwise unchanged: on the contrary, it changes everything. To start with, the human self and finite being have to be completely re-thought—as does also morality.

I am the sort of person for whom ideas are like living beings, hugely powerful forces that can erupt violently within one's psyche. I had to move slowly; and in any case I did not get tenure as a university lecturer until 1976, when I was already forty-two. Until then, it was not safe to speak; but thereafter I came out quite quickly. I was a contributor to *The Myth of God Incarnate* in 1977, and published *Taking Leave of God*, in which I first declared explicitly for the non-realist view of God, in 1980. This latter book was instantly denounced as "atheism" on all sides, despite the fact that I had taken care to include in it a few phrases that kept it just within the bounds of the old high orthodoxy of the Negative Theology. The church and the theology faculties were not aware that non-realism is a technical term in philosophy, and they still regard it as sim-ply a euphemism for sheer and shameless unbelief.

The present collection includes papers of various kinds from the period 1980–2000. It begins with "Kant and the

Negative Theology" (chapter 1), which was the very last statement of my old position before I came out as a non-realist.
It was contributed to the Donald MacKinnon Festschrift, *The
Philosophical Frontiers of Christian Theology*, eds. Brian Hebblethwaite and Stewart Sutherland (Cambridge: The Cambridge University Press, 1982).

There follow three of the many papers in which I have from
time to time tried to explain the non-realist understanding
of religious belief. Chapter 2, "Faith Alone," was written in
1984–85 for Peter Eaton, ed., *The Trial of Faith* (Worthing, England: Churchman Publishing, 1988). Chapter 3, "Anti-Realist
Faith," was written for a conference organized by John Hick
and held in Los Angeles at the Claremont Group of Colleges
early in 1988. The full proceedings appeared in Joseph Runzo,
ed., *Is God Real?* (London and New York: Macmillan, 1993).
Chapter 4, "Free Christianity," was written for *God and Reality: Essays on Christian Non-realism*, ed. Colin Crowder (London
and New York: Mowbray/Cassell, 1977).

The next group of papers, Part 3, is titled "The Practice of
Post-Dogmatic Religion." It begins with Chapter 5, "Is Anything Sacred?," which was written for the third national conference of Sea of Faith (UK) in 1990, and was published in
the journal *Religious Humanism*, ed. Mason Olds, Vol. 24, No.
4 (Autumn 1990). The lecture deals with the seeming eclipse
of the sacred in the modern world, and looks at the move
toward nihilism in religion and in modern art. Because I have
written a good deal about the history of painting over the past
150 years or so, and (like Mark C. Taylor) have emphasized its
great religious significance, I have been very pleased to find a
number of artists among those who like my ideas.

Chapter 6, "The Human Condition: Diagnosis and Ther-
apy," is the Sea of Faith (UK) lecture for the next year, 1991.
It moves in a Christian Buddhist direction, and I offered it to
Satish Kumar, the editor of *Resurgence* magazine, when he
asked for a piece. It appeared in the issue for March/April
1993, and was subsequently reprinted in *Only Connect: Soil,
Soul and Society*, eds. John Lane and Maya Kumar Mitchell
(Totnes, Devon: Green Books, 2000). Chapter 7, "Spirituality,

Old and New," was written for the eleventh conference of Sea
of Faith (UK), and is about going "solar." The move to non-
realism implies abandoning not just metaphysics, but there-
with also the soul and life after death—which means in turn
that we discard the old introvertive spirituality of purifying
one's soul in preparation for the next life, and we go all out for
an extravertive, solar, expressive spirituality of *this* life. Here I
am at my most Nietzschean, but it took me a while to grasp
all the implications of the fact that when this life becomes
our very *last* life, we are forced to move on from ecclesiastical
theology to kingdom theology. The old spirituality was designed for people who expected another and better world after
death. They were *in via*, on the way. Their religion was disciplinary and preparatory: but we, we are *already in* the very last
world we will ever know. So we've got to go for the final religious goal, eternal life, here and now. Non-realism thus continues the project of the Radical Reformation.

Chapter 8, "The Radical Christian Worldview," was written
in 1998–99 for a multifaith symposium that (like so many sym-
posia) never appeared. All the writers were given the same
little group of questions, to be answered as candidly as possible: hence the form of my piece, which was eventually published in the fiftieth anniversary issue of the American journal
Cross Currents, Vol. 50, Nos. 1–2 (La Rochelle, NY: Spring/
Summer 2000). The journal is published by the Association
for Religion and Intellectual Life (ARIL).

The two essays in Part 4 are headed "The Turn to Life."
Having a strong interest in natural science, I have often been
asked to write about environmental questions and "Green
Theology." It has never been an easy topic to say something
either philosophically or theologically new about, and I have
had only one good line of thought. It has to do with the meaning and use of the word "life," which includes both biological
life *(bios)* and our human communicative social life *(zoe)*.
Chapter 9, "The Value of Life," was written for the seventy-
seventh annual conference of The Modern Churchpeople's
Union, held at Hoddesdon, Hertfordshire, in 1989, and published in the journal *The Modern Churchman* NS., Vol. 32, No. 2

(1990). So far as I can remember, the paper was not very well received, but as I now read it again I am pleased with it. It does recognize the urgent need to rethink *life*, after Darwin, after Nietzsche, and in the light of the turn to life that has taken place in twentieth-century thought. Chapter 10, "Nature and Culture," was a Centenary Gifford Lecture, written in 1991 and delivered at Glasgow University. It shows me trying to update the traditional Nature/Culture contrast in the light of modern French thought. It was first published in Neil Spurway, ed., *Humanity, Environment and God* (Oxford and Cambridge, Mass.: Blackwell, 1993). I should add that these lines of thought about life came to fruition in *The New Religion of Life in Everyday Speech* (London: SCM Press, 1999).

Finally, in Part 5 are a couple of brief pieces that show me replying to critics. It is sometimes said that there has not been enough dialogue between me and my contemporaries. This has happened partly because I have been excluded from consideration because of my views, and partly because I have been so frantically busy. During the period 1980–2000, I was a full-time university lecturer, a college dean, and the holder of three other college posts. I was very active in the media, published twenty-two books, and lectured at all Sea of Faith conferences. I also managed to fit in something involuntary, namely many years of poor mental health. So I have been preoccupied, but the two replies to critics reprinted here are included because they contain some worthwhile material. "A Reply to Rowan Williams" was first published in the journal *Modern Theology*, Vol. 1, No. 1 (October 1984), following an article by him entitled "Religious Realism: On Not Quite Agreeing with Don Cupitt." It was written at a moment of transition in my own thinking: I was still rather voluntaristic in a left-Kierkegaardian kind of way, but was becoming very enthusiastic about modern French thought, and about Derrida in particular. I have never been a good follower of anybody, and I have never written at length about anybody else; but I did during the 1980s gain a valuable stimulus from French thought, and perhaps especially from Mark C. Taylor's *Erring*

(University of Chicago Press, 1984), the book that first and most eloquently spelled out its theological implications.

Finally, chapter 12 is "A Reply to David Edwards," which was first published in his *Tradition and Truth: The Challenge of England's Radical Theologians 1962–1989* (London: Hodder and Stoughton, 1989). The book is not exactly weighty, but for thirty years or so, David Edwards had been the principal reviewer for the Anglican weekly, *The Church Times*. His reviews always came first, and from an immense height of assumed intellectual and moral superiority: he formulated the church's corporate response to our works, and by and large the Establishment followed the line he laid down. So naturally I wanted to retort that non-realism is not very difficult to understand, and that there really is a great need for church reform. Both intellectually and morally, the church is in big trouble. But it refuses to acknowledge the fact, as it still refuses to understand non-realism.

Looking at the dates on the Contents page, you will see that most of these papers come from the period of my most intense activity in the middle and late 1980s. Earlier, in the period 1980 to early 1984, all my spare time was taken up with producing the Sea of Faith book and documentary film series. Later, from 1991, health problems forced a gradual withdrawal from church activity, from university teaching, and from public controversy. One by one, I gave up all my jobs and got down to writing books—producing twelve in the period 1990–1999, whereas there had been only eight in the previous decade and nine in the 1970s.

The main aim in this most recent period has been to push my thinking through to a new stage. I felt that I should escape from relatively ephemeral controversies and instead try to press on with a larger task—the Nietzschean revolution in religious thought that had long been my underlying aim. Why so many books? people complained. My best answer was to point to another analogy with painting: I wanted to *show the working*. In nineteenth-century art, some painters would put immense labor into producing a few very big and highly-finished academic paintings of a kind that completely concealed the work that had gone into them. But Constable's sketches are in many ways more interesting than his academic paintings, and from the first "Impressionist" exhibition in 1874 onward, painters worked fast, and exhibited paintings in which all the work is left visible. You can see *exactly* how Monet does light on water. I liked that: so I aimed for a similar effect. I scorned laborious, scholarly, academic work: I aimed to write fast and take risks. I took no pains to achieve consistency by re-reading my earlier books, preferring each time to start as if afresh, working at very high temperature, choosing new terminology if I could, and leaving my workings showing. Apart from *The Sea of Faith* (1984), nearly all my books have been (admittedly, much corrected) first drafts. The point of this was, and is, that I have been trying to reinvent religious thought: I believed that I ought to show as explicitly as I could how it was being done. Unlike Nietzsche, I have wanted to *democratize* creative thinking—the remote scriptural influence behind this ambition being Moses's cry: "Would God that all the Lord's people were prophets!" (Numbers 11:29).

My democratic hopes have not so far won me much applause, because most of the world consists of people who either regard all religion as irrational, so that "religious thought" is an oxymoron; or think that in religion the truth is already known, so that religious thought is completely unnecessary. I was much disconcerted to meet one of these latter folk very recently: a cathedral in the South-East of England had rather bravely invited me to lecture on the non-realist view of God. So I turned up and performed, quite well, I fancied—but then I was thrown by an elderly member of the audience who, for the life of her, could not understand what I was up to. "Look here," she said, "I go to church, I say my prayers, I keep the rules. Before long I'll die in faith and go to Heaven. It's all perfectly straightforward. What are you on about? Why do you make all these unnecessary difficulties? What good do you think you can possibly be doing?" There was no place in her world-view for a person like me or for religious thought, and I felt somewhat stumped. How could I justify my existence to someone like her?

That is rather like the paradoxical question of how non-realism is to be explained. There is no extra-human, extra-linguistic, but intelligible, order out there to be successfully captured and represented in my writing; there is no revealed standard vocabulary that gets it all just right, and no best order of exposition, either. Therefore, there can be no such thing as an accurate statement of non-realist doctrine. So what am I going to do about that? No wonder Mary Warnock is cross with me: she's right, and I can't answer her back.

A friend who is acutely aware of these problems, Hilary Lawson, has just published what is perhaps the first large-scale Anglo-Saxon non-realist "metaphysics," *Closure* (London and New York: Routledge, 2001). As he puts it, for 2000 years we have believed in the possibility of a single true account of the world. Recently, that belief has run into difficulties so acute that it seems that we must give up the traditional correspondence theory of truth and the belief in a pre-existing and ready-made world out there. Instead we should regard the world as open and indeterminate, but as (perhaps) very dense with waiting possibilities. It is then we who close the world, determine it, form it, by our stories. Of course, the number of different possible closures is indefinitely large, and so far probably only a very small fraction of them have been checked out.

Now Hilary Lawson has specialized in the pervasive problem of reflexivity, and he is well aware of the fact that his argument must apply to itself. If the world is *that* open, he can't prove non-realism *true* (for there is nothing for it to be true *of*), nor can he claim that his account of it is the best that can be given. So he subtitles his book not *the theory of every-thing*, but *a story of everything*, just one among many other stories of everything that wait to be told.

That's too thin, and during the past ten years or so, I have tried various dodges for luring and enticing the reader into a sudden revelation of the strange non-truth of non-realism. The best is an attempt to prove, or at least force the reader to agree, that all propositional thought consists in a motion of language. I force the admission chiefly by saying: What the hell *else* could it be?[6] But if all meaningful thought is couched in language, the truth of non-realism quickly follows. For consider: (1) If all (meaningful, propositional) thought is dependent upon language, then our whole experience and knowledge of the world is always-already coded into language. (2) The world then comes to be, takes shape and is world *only* in our description of it. (3) But we, we are the only speakers, the only fully-conscious beings, the only beings who have a proper *world*, at all! Only in the "brightness" of our description and conscious knowledge of it, then, is the world *the world*. (4) Therefore non-realism is (sort-of) true. There is now only one point to add, which is that we humans are part of the world, and can know ourselves, and *be* ourselves, only in the language we use to describe ourselves. Thus my non-realist pataphysics[7] has to be called not just radical humanism, but "*Empty* radical humanism." There are no substances or real beings knowable outside language, and that statement applies to *us*, as well as to our world.

That is one very recent attempt to take non-realism further, and develop it into a strong new doctrine that can be taught and believed without impossible paradoxicality. Alas, I don't think it's going to please my distinguished critics! Another attempt was made in the patacartesian argument of *The Last Philosophy* (1995). Here I began by asking what there is whose existence cannot be denied without absurdity, and the answer was of course *not* the thinking subject, but simply language. From which everything else soon follows.

Non-realism, however, remains unpopular. Most philosophers are still scornful, but the very great success of Richard Rorty's neo-pragmatism and "non-representationalism" (his version of non-realism) suggests that the tide may yet turn, even in benighted old Britain. The difficulty I have found with theologians is that they want philosophy only for instrumental purposes: they will take bits of philosophy where they

---

[6] See my "Thinking in Words," in *Creation Out of Nothing* (Philadelphia: Trinity Press International and London: SCM Press, 1990), pp. 157–166.

[7] The College of Pataphysics was a long-running joke-entity in Paris 40-odd years ago.

see it as helping them to explain and justify their doctrines, but they are very suspicious of big philosophical ideas. Perhaps they are right: perhaps my own utter delight in big, dizzy, dangerous philosophy has harmed me in every way. But it is an addiction I can't give up now.

One further consequence of non-realism deserves to be spelled out. It could encourage a revival of utopian thinking. Among political conservatives it is often said that we can't change things for the better because unyielding Laws of God, of Nature, of "the market," or facts about human nature stand in our way. Non-realists reply that we ourselves generated among ourselves our own pictures of God, of the natural order, of human nature, and we devised our own economic system. What we made, we can reinvent. Thus in a period when all the old progressive ideologies have died, non-realism may encourage a revival of much-needed dreams of a better world (and of a better religion, too, by the way). This line of thinking has been proposed by some of the French, such as Lyotard and Deleuze, and in the U.S. by Richard Rorty in his more recent writings. In my own work, the same move is made by my claim that in order to renew Christianity, we now have to move it on from its disciplinary ecclesiastical form to its final and fully-realized "Kingdom" form.[8]

I must thank Professor John D. Caputo for kindly suggesting that I should contribute something to this series.

Don Cupitt
Cambridge 2002

---

[8] *Reforming Christianity* (Santa Rosa: Polebridge Press, 2001).

1
On the Brink

1

Kant and the
Negative Theology

DONALD MACKINNON has described Kant's religious thought
as standing in the tradition of the negative theology.[1]

There is an obvious truth in this. By the negative theology
we usually understand the doctrine that so emphasizes God's
transcendence as to remove him beyond the reach of descriptive language. God cannot be characterized directly but only
indirectly, by saying that he is not subject to the limits that
make other objects capturable in language. Thus it is said that
God is not-limited, not-dependent, not-bodily, not-temporal,
not-spatial, not-complex, and so forth.

Sometimes the doctrine is misunderstood as asserting that
all judgements about God must be negative in their grammati-
cal form; and then the objection is made that every negation
implies a corresponding affirmation, so that the doctrine de-
feats itself. For surely, to *deny* that God is complex and temporal is to *affirm* that God is simple and eternal. However, this is
not quite the point. The main emphasis is not upon grammati-
cal negatives, but rather upon the necessarily indirect character of all language about God. The motive was originally
reverential. The ancient Jews evolved a great variety of pe-
riphrases and similar constructions to avoid speaking directly
of God, and the negative theology is simply a hellenized version of the same practice.

An analogy may help to make the point clear. A short list of
categorical negative commandments is a rather generous ethical code, for it leaves a great deal of scope for creative choice

---

[1] D. M. MacKinnon, *The Problem of Metaphysics* (Cambridge, 1974), p. 9;
"Kant's Philosophy of Religion," *Philosophy*, L (1975), p. 141.

in positive action. By contrast, a short list of categorical af-
firmative commandments leaves much less choice. Somewhat
similarly, a habit of speaking of God in an indirect or veiled
way leaves a great deal of logical space for God to move in. It
does not pretend to restrict God, but preserves a decent reti-
cence. The obliqueness of the language bears witness to the
transcendence of that to which it alludes.

The Greek goes beyond the Jew only in that he says, in
rather more express terms, that it is not merely religiously presumptuous to try to pin God down in human language, but
logically impossible. For God is strictly ineffable or incomprehensible.

Many of the Greek Fathers quoted texts from Plato that
they took to support this view, such as the assertion in the
Republic (509b) that the Good is "beyond being." Since Being
was commonly thought to be the most general of the categories, and that in which all the others inhere, to describe the
Good as beyond being is to imply that it eludes all the categories, and therefore altogether transcends human comprehen-
sion.[2] Kant's doctrine is rather similar, for he holds that the
categories of the understanding are simply rules for ordering
experience. Within the world of experience we can define criteria for applying these rules so as to generate objective
knowledge; but the categories cannot have any proper transcendent application beyond the bounds of possible experience. Apart from experience and the criteria for applying them
in experience, they are empty. So the categories of substance,
causality, and so forth cannot profitably be extrapolated beyond the world. There can be no valid causal inference from
the world to its unknown ground, and there is no way of en-
larging our knowledge of the unknowable world-ground by
analogical reasoning. For Kant, David Hume had exposed the
arbitrariness and futility of that kind of anthropomorphism.

Hume himself had ended with a theism reduced to vanish-
ing-point: "The cause or causes of order in the universe probably bear some remote analogy to human intelligence," but

---

[2] G. C. Stead, *Divine Substance* (Oxford, 1977), p. 140.

that proposition is not capable of any further elaboration, and can have no practical consequences.[3] Kant took a different view. He still held a form of the old belief that the idea of God is innate in human reason. The mind is naturally oriented towards God, spontaneously generates the idea of God, and needs that idea. Yet on the speculative side, Kant's view of God is, if possible, still more austere than Hume's, for he holds that there is no way at all of moving from our idea of God to God's actual being. His solution was to say that *our idea of God* (the Ideal of Reason) has a valuable regulative function to perform both in guiding theoretical reason and as a postulate of practical reason, always provided that we fully recognize its speculative inadequacy. So, unlike Hume, Kant certainly did not wish belief in God to become inoperative and practically insignificant. He believed it was essential to retain it, and held that the idea of God can indeed be kept provided that we use it merely as a rule for guiding our thought and action within this world, and do not pretend to gain thereby any speculative knowledge of the unknowable world-ground. Yet in a strange way, the very strenuousness with which Kant strives to remain within the limits of thought, and his insistence on our inability to know God as God is, may itself be seen as an indirect or "negative" witness to the Transcendent.

So in these two respects there is a real resemblance between what Kant is saying and the old tradition of the negative theology, though we are already beginning to notice some differences emerging. Kant is himself, and not a Greek Father. When we inquire in more detail into just what is meant by the negative theology, complications arise. Kant actually seems to *contradict* many of its main tenets, and though there will remain a broad truth in the claim that we who live after Kant must walk the negative way, it will certainly not be quite the same way as it was for the classical theologians. Many of the old landmarks have gone.

---

[3] D. Hume, *Dialogues Concerning Natural Religion* (1779), 12, ed. Henry D. Aiken (New York, 1948), p. 94 (italics removed).

What, then, was the negative theology? The best reply is
that it was a set of doctrines, a temper of mind, and a style
of spirituality very widespread among theologians (including
Platonists, Christians, Jews, and, eventually, Muslims also) for
over a thousand years. Understood in a broad sense, it is still
an essential feature of mainstream orthodox theism, especially
in the Greek Orthodox tradition because of the special authority that tradition gives to the Cappadocian Fathers, the
Pseudo-Dionysius, and St. John of Damascus.

In this old high-orthodox theism, one of the most commonly recurring assertions runs as follows: it is certain that
God exists, but the nature or essence of God is unknowable.
The mystery may be invoked by speaking of it indirectly, or
in negations, or by affirming symbolic "names;" but in the
end it is ungraspable by the mind, as the eye is dazzled by the
sun.

A few examples of this assertion may be quoted. Philo, writing about A.D. 20–40, says that God "is not apprehensible by
the mind, save in the fact that he is. For it is his existence
which we apprehend, and of what lies outside that existence,
nothing."[4] In the fourth century, St. Basil says, "That God is,
I know; but what is his essence I hold to be above reason."[5]
Thomas Aquinas, in the thirteenth century, discusses the nature of God under three headings; his existence, "what manner of being he is, or rather, what manner of being he is not,"
and his activity.[6] As late as the eighteenth century, we still
find Hume's *Dialogues* being conducted upon the premise formulated by Pamphilus and Demea: God's existence is certain,
but his nature is at least problematic, and for Demea it is "altogether incomprehensible and unknown to us."[7] It is still
Demea, not Cleanthes, who is described as orthodox.

Modern philosophy, having been to school with Hume,
Kant, and Frege, finds this old doctrine empty and foolish.
The basic objection was clearly formulated by the deist John

---

[4] Philo, *Quod Deus Immutabilis Sit*, 62.

[5] St. Basil, *Epistle* 234.

[6] Thomas Aquinas, *Summa Theologiae*, Ia, prologue to Question 2.

[7] Hume, *Dialogues*, foreword and part 2, *ad init.*

Toland: "Could that Person justly value himself upon being wiser than his Neighbours, who having infallible assurance that something call'd *Blictri* had a being in Nature, in the mean time knew not what this Blictri was?"[8]

Toland is surely right. The affirmation that God exists has no content unless something can be said about what God is. From the modern point of view, Thomas Aquinas seems in the following text merely to be striving after vacuity: "In this life our minds cannot grasp what God is in himself; whatever way we have of thinking of him is a way of failing to understand him as he really is. So the less determinate our names are and the more general and simple they are, the more appropriately they may be applied to God."[9] Surely this amounts to saying, the vaguer the better, even unto perfect emptiness?

Kant, of course, fully accepts that the old doctrine has collapsed, and for him it is God's *existence* rather than his nature that is unknowable. God's *nature* is not mysterious, for we have a clear, unproblematic and useful *idea* of God immanent within our reason. Kant is very bold on this point. In *Prolegomena*[10] he says that many things given to us in experience, such as gravitational attraction, are utterly mysterious to us; but when we step outside nature we deal with mere concepts generated by our own reason, and they are not mysterious at all, for Reason can certainly explain its own products. It spontaneously produces the idea of God and uses it to guide the understanding towards the ideal of the completest possible systematic unity in our scientific explanation of the world. As for the use of the idea of God in ethics, Kant says in the *Religion*[11] that "every man *creates a God* for himself, nay, must make himself such a God according to moral concepts." For if

---

[8] J. Toland, *Christianity Not Mysterious* (1696), p. 133. The growth of discontent with the old doctrine that God's existence is certain but his nature unknowable is described in Don Cupitt, "The Doctrine of Analogy in the Age of Locke," *JTS*, n.s. 19 (1968), pp. 186–202.

[9] Aquinas, *ST*, Ia, 13, 11.

[10] P. G. Lucas, ed. and trans., Kant's *Prolegomena*, § 56 (Manchester, 1953), pp. 114f.

[11] T. M. Greene and H. H. Hudson, trans., *Religion within the Limits of Reason Alone* (New York, 1960), p. 175n.

someone presents us with something and urges us to worship it, we must refuse. Kant insists on the insufficiency of any empirical or inductive approach to theology, warns against the danger of heteronomy, and holds that what God is for us and what faith is must be purely rationally determined. It would be idolatry to acknowledge any other God than the God who is immanent in practical reason.

It sounds as if at this point Kant is deliberately setting out to contradict the element of authoritarian appeal to mystery in the old negative theology. On the contrary, he says, the nature of God must be comprehensible, for the concept of God is generated by human reason. It guides the understanding and inspires moral endeavor. But of course for Kant, the actuality of God can never be given in experience, and we can therefore never be theoretically justified in asserting either God's existence or God's non-existence. On Kant's account God's existence is problematic, but God's nature *as the Ideal of Reason* is explicable; and he adds that the ultimate world-ground must remain unknowable.

Thus, although Kant does continue some of the themes of the old negative theology, he alters it considerably in order to make it intellectually and morally more acceptable. The old doctrine asserted that God's existence is certain but his nature unknowable. For Kant the proofs of God's existence fail, and the old doctrine is in any case empty and morally objectionable. In his view, acceptance of a positive revelation of suprarational truth would subject us to an odious *despotism of mystery*. The Ideal of Reason is an available God who is intellectually and morally acceptable, and we must preserve strict agnosticism about the real God.

In retrospect we find ourselves asking the question, "Why did not the old theologians see that they were talking nonsense in asserting both that God's existence is certain and that we can know nothing of what God is? For seventeen centuries this assertion was copied from one writer to another, and they all thought it was true until Toland came along and showed it to be empty in one sentence. Why?"

The answer is surely that in prescientific culture, before the

Enlightenment, the universe was commonly perceived as a hierarchy of powers or energies. To say that a thing existed was to attribute to it a certain degree of activity, life, or power, and therefore a certain status in the cosmic hierarchy of powers. So the Old Testament prophets typically say of pagan gods that they are *weak*. It was not usual to say that Bel or Nebo did not exist. It was sufficient to say that Bel and Nebo did not have the power-rank their devotees misguidedly attributed to them.

With this view of existence as the most general descriptive predicate went the doctrine of degrees of being, and the various maxims about causality. Everything in the universe is empowered, energized, and caused to exist by something else that is above it in rank. Every effect has a cause, the cause (since it is something of higher rank in the order of being) has in itself in a more eminent way all the qualities that are found in the effect, and so on.

The universe was therefore conceived as a descending power-hierarchy. Everything comes down from above. Such a system, it was thought, clearly must have an apex, and the purpose of the ancient emphasis on God's transcendence was to insist that the apex was not the Heavens, nor astral deities, but a God enthroned above the Heavens who transcended the cosmos altogether. To speak of God in negations was not to empty the concept of God but rather positively to affirm the plenitude of God's sovereign unlimited freedom and originating power.[12] Similarly, to call God pure act, or pure existence, or He Who Is, did not seem empty: on the contrary, it was to affirm his supreme omnipresent power and activity.

The old negative way thus belonged with, and was intelligible in terms of, a certain view of the universe that has now passed away. It is not difficult to show, as Anthony Kenny does,[13] the emptiness of its slogans in terms of the modern analysis of existence as the exemplification of a concept. The modern negative theology, after Kant, has to endure objective

---

[12] G. L. Prestige, *God in Patristic Thought* (London, 1956 edition), pp. 4ff.
[13] A. Kenny, *The Five Ways* (London, 1969).

uncertainty about the existence of God. There are many ways of trying to cope with this but, however one copes with it, it is a new situation.

When we turn to the related question of causality, we again find that Kantian theism is somewhat different from the old tradition.

The earliest Jewish monotheism said something like this: the reality of God is undeniable and inescapable. God is a massive and dreadful concentration of pure sacred power by which society lives and on whose favor its well-being depends. God is too terrible for any but the most outstanding holy men to be able to approach him directly. It is either forbidden or impossible to see God: but though God cannot be grasped directly, his intentions and his will are revealed in the word of law and prophecy.

As these ideas were formalized in the theology of much later times, they were expressed thus: God certainly exists, God is equally certainly unknowable, but there is an indirect knowledge of God through his works of Creation, Revelation, and so on. In some modern theology it has been claimed that God reveals himself; but this was not usually said in earlier times, for if it were said, it would violate the basic principle of the negative theology. It is not himself that God reveals, but his will and purposes, what we are to do, how creatures depend upon him, and so on. Thus Aquinas says: "From divine effects we do not come to understand what the divine nature is in itself, so we do not know of God what he is."[14]

This last point is important. The traditional theology was, or was usually, cautious in its claims. Put at its most cautious, it was *not* claiming that beginning from worldly events you could reason back (by analogy and the causal maxims) to gain a real knowledge of the divine nature: but it was claiming that the world itself and some particular events in the world can be *recognized as God's effects*.

However, even that minimal claim is still somewhat more than Kant will allow. He vetoes any attempt to enlarge our

---

[14] Aquinas, *ST*, Ia, 13, 8.

knowledge by causal inference from the world to God; and although he does have a place for analogy, he always interprets it as a way of ordering our worldly knowledge and action, and not as, in any sense, describing God. There may be some thought-guiding value in regarding certain features of the world *as if* they were God's effects, but we are not entitled to say flatly that they *are* so.

In the *Prolegomena*,[15] Kant makes the point by distinguishing between dogmatic and symbolic anthropomorphism. When we say that God is the world-maker, we are saying something about how we are impelled to regard the world, namely, *as if* it were the work of a highest understanding and will. Such symbolic anthropomorphism has regulative value, but we must not pretend that it adds to our knowledge of God as he is in himself. The analogy of God as world-designer is a way of ordering our understanding of the world, and no more.

In the *Religion* [16] Kant makes the same point by distinguishing between a schematism of analogy and an analogy of objective determination. To understand a biological organism, I must think of it as if it had been designed. Given the limits of human understanding, I cannot fully reconcile mechanistic and teleological methods of explanation; perhaps only God can know the world in a way that synthesizes them. What I have to do is use mechanistic explanation, supplemented by a purely regulative use of teleological explanation. But this is a fact about how my mind works, and it does not justify me in positively asserting that the unknown world-cause itself must possess intelligence. To say so would lead at once to the anthropomorphism that Hume has so effectively attacked. Again, Kant allows our talk of God an intra-mundane use, but he will not allow it an extra-mundane reference.

The same is also true of Kant's discussions of the distinction between a discursive and an intuitive understanding. The object of making the distinction is to reveal the character and the limits of the human understanding, not to gain speculative

---

[15] I. Kant, *Prolegomena*, Lucas edition, §§ 57–58, pp. 116–28.
[16] Kant (Lucas), pp. 58ff.

knowledge of the Divine Mind.[17] Kant is so fascinated by the idea of an intuitive understanding that we might even say that for him, the human mind cannot become fully conscious of itself except by measuring itself against an idea of the Divine Mind. That may be true, but it is still only a fact about *us*, and cannot for Kant be made the basis of an epistemological proof of God's existence, or of claims to an innate knowledge of God.

Thirdly, we may consider Kant's attitude to another theme of the traditional negative theology, which goes back to Philo and perhaps even to Plato. It was said that God is the One, the Monad beyond all distinctions, like a point which has position but no magnitude. God is unknowable by the ordinary apparatus of human understanding. In short, God can only be known by an ecstasy of reason. Various examples of this ecstasy of reason may be quoted: revelation, prophetic inspiration, or the receptive and passive unknowing of the mystic.[18]

It scarcely needs saying that Kant's whole theory of knowledge and temper of mind are unfriendly to such an idea, but there is a brief passage in the *Religion*[19] where he says something about mysticism. Interestingly, the subject provokes him to one of his very rare recognitions that the principles governing the objectivity of human knowledge need to be established publicly or communally. In so far as mystical experience is private, it is mysterious and of no theoretical or cognitive import, for to have such import, "it would have to be capable of being shared with everyone and made known publicly." "Feelings are not knowledge," says Kant, reminding us of the way Russell and Wittgenstein were later to distinguish between science and mysticism.[20]

Kant does recognize that there is indeed a holy mystery at

---

[17] C. D. Broad, *Kant: An Introduction*, ed. C. Lewy (Cambridge, 1978), pp. 309ff.

[18] See H. Chadwick's chapters in *The Cambridge History of Later Greek and Early Medieval Philosophy*, ed. A. H. Armstrong (Cambridge, 1967).

[19] Kant (Lucas), pp. 129ff.

[20] For example, the title essay in B. Russell, *Mysticism and Logic* (London, 1918); and L. Wittgenstein, *Tractatus Logico-Philosophicus*, trans. D. F. Pears and B. F. McGuinness (London, 1961), §§ 6.4ff.

the center of religious faith. It is a private matter, and not of public or theoretical value; but it is more than just a matter of feeling, for since it is holy it must be moral and so an object of reason. It must be thought of as emerging from our inner moral predisposition. And so Kant is led back to the postulates of practical reason, to the mystery of freedom, to our duty to pursue the highest good, and to our need to believe in God as the condition of the attainability of the highest good. In the end, "this belief really contains no mystery."[21] By this, Kant means that rational faith in God as Lawgiver and Judge, rightly understood as being merely regulative and as derived from reason itself and not from any external authority, is unmysterious.

Kant continues to say that there remains a mystery beyond our grasp. There is much we cannot know; but we must not be *seduced* by the unknowable. Awareness of the limits of thought must strengthen, not weaken, our resolve to live autonomously by the light we actually have. Thus, we know nothing at all about God's providential government of the world, and cannot conceive how God may be able to bring nature into line with the demands of morality. But we can safely leave that problem to look after itself: "it may well be expedient for us merely to know and understand that there is such a mystery, not to comprehend it."[22]

This rules out theodicy as an enterprise that is both beyond our powers and morally unnecessary. Joseph Butler, fifty years earlier, had still believed that we could point out some empirical signs of God's moral government of the world. Belief in providence is to some extent confirmed in our moral experience, even though the whole scheme is very imperfectly comprehended. Butler, an honest man, had spun the argument very fine, but nevertheless he still claimed that the workings of providence are empirically detectable.[23] Kant abandons that claim, and as he does so we can see him once again separating

---

[21] Kant (Lucas), p. 131.
[22] Ibid., p. 130n.
[23] J. Butler, *The Analogy of Religion* (1736), part 1.

religion into two halves. There is the part that concerns us, which is unmysterious, rational, and moral; our duty, practical reason, and its postulates: and there is the part that does not concern us because it is a mystery into which we cannot penetrate. It is sufficient to acknowledge the mystery. In Kant's view we must not allow ourselves to heed the siren voices of those who say that because the ultimate is mysterious, we must therefore accept the claims of revelation, church authority, religious irrationalism, and mysticism. Instead he offers a way of faith that makes no concessions to such things.

At this point, what Kant is saying is strikingly different from the older negative theology, which had always been closely allied with mysticism. The Greek Fathers, for example, invoke a sense of the mystery of the divine transcendence in order to awaken heavenly longings. Their language is designed to *attract*, whereas Kant's language is designed to *repel*. Kant wants us to renounce impossible and futile aspirations and be content with doing our duty. Do not aspire after the real God, he says, for that will only end in anthropomorphism and fantasy. Be content with the available God postulated by practical reason—fully recognizing his non-descriptive character—for that is sufficient. The nearest you can come to the real God lies in your very recognition of the merely regulative status of the notion of God with which in fact you must operate. It is vain and morally harmful to ask for more.

The old negative way was speculative and mystical, whereas Kant's purpose is to eliminate speculative and mystical theology. In this life, the only way to God is the path of duty, and the traditional task of theodicy, to

> . . . assert Eternal Providence.
> And justify the ways of God to men.

is ruled out as impossible.

This reminds us of another context in which the phrase "negative theology" is used, and one that is well known to be of interest to Donald MacKinnon. To many of his early readers, Kant seemed pessimistic and skeptical. An interesting case is that of the writer Heinrich von Kleist, who was overwhelmed by what he learnt of the Kantian philosophy in the years 1800–1801. It broke his faith in the possibility of steady progress by self-cultivation toward the ideal of absolute knowledge of the whole truth of things. Kant seemed to have destroyed the optimistic world-view of the Enlightenment. It appeared that all we can ever know is the truth as constructed by us from appearances. We can never know the truth absolutely. By asserting that the pure ego was unknowable, Kant had set impassable limits to self-knowledge, and by separating morality from nature he had eliminated any objectively sustained meaning or moral order in the course of human life as we empirically live it. In a series of eight cold stories, Kleist shows a world in which there is no moral providence, life makes no sense, fate is amoral, ironical, or malicious, and people cannot understand the truth of their own or other people's behavior.[24] In a letter, Kleist hopes that, in spite of the evidence, the world is not governed by an evil spirit, but merely by one who is not understood. Kleist committed suicide in 1811 at the age of 34.

Kleist, it is said, misunderstood Kant. But Kant himself, after all, had "found it necessary to deny *knowledge*, in order to make room for *faith*."[25] Kant allows us no knowledge of God's real existence, nature or action, and no built-in, empirically-detectable and sustaining moral providence in the empirical world. Rejecting the possibility of mystical knowledge of God by an ecstasy of reason, Kant is left with a non-cognitive philosophy of religion which leaves the believer to be sustained in a harsh world by nothing but pure moral faith. Though it can truly be said that Kant's religious views are in the tradition of the negative way, I suggest that our discussion has shown that his position is more bleak and austere than that of any of his predecessors.

In the recent debates in Britain, a number of writers, including R. B. Braithwaite, R. M. Hare, T. R. Miles, and D. Z.

---

[24] Heinrich von Kleist, *The Marquise of O— and other Stories* (1810–11), trans. David Luke and Nigel Reeves (Harmondsworth, 1978).

[25] I. Kant, *Critique of Pure Reason*, B 30, trans. Norman Kemp Smith (London, 1933), p. 29.

Phillips, have proposed various forms of non-cognitive philosophy of religion.[26] Their views are interestingly varied, and it may well be urged that Phillips in particular is a writer of genuine religious force, who shows what form the negative way must take in our time, and who, through Wittgenstein and Kierkegaard, stands in the tradition that flows from Kant.

Phillips, of course, differs from Kant. He does not claim, and few nowadays would wish to claim, that the idea of God is necessary to motivate scientific endeavor; for why should not the ideal of the greatest possible systematic unity and completeness in our scientific theory of the world be an autonomous ideal? For many, it clearly is so. Nor does Phillips agree with Kant's drastic subordination of religion to morality, for he regards religion as an autonomous and irreducible way of speaking, acting, and appraising one's life. On the other hand, those who think Kant's view of religion very impoverished should note that he conserves certain important religious values perhaps better than Phillips does. For Kant has an eschatology, a pilgrim sense of life in which our present endeavors are sustained by the hope of a glorious consummation yet to come.

Still, Kant and Phillips have much in common. Both philosophies of religion are (in the modern jargon) non-cognitive. Both go further, and declare that all objectification in religious thought is a temptation to be resisted. No doubt many people do suppose that religious doctrines describe real invisible beings, occult agencies, and supernatural events that both underlie and are interwoven with the world of fact. But if that is what they think, then they are superstitious; and modern philosophy, in exposing their error, purifies faith. Accordingly Phillips, in particular, refuses to go on the defensive and refuses to admit that his view is reductionist.

Phillips's remarkable philosophy of religion may represent one form the ancient discipline of the negative way might take

---

[26] For Braithwaite and Hare, see *The Philosophy of Religion*, ed. Basil Mitchell (Oxford, 1971), pp. 72–91, 15–19; T. R. Miles, *Religion and the Scientific Outlook* (London, 1959); D. Z. Phillips, *Faith and Philosophical Enquiry* (London, 1970).

in our time. Donald MacKinnon, though, takes a very different view. He insists on sticking to a descriptivist or realist interpretation of the major themes of traditional Christian theology.[27] He thinks one should stay with and endure the peculiarly intractable intellectual difficulties that such a position involves. He admires such a stark presentation of the problem of evil as Kleist gives in his story "The Earthquake in Chile." To face the facts of evil and tragedy and the trial of faith to which they subject us is itself (though in a very different sense from that of Phillips) to walk in "the negative way." For MacKinnon, I believe, the true negative way is the Way of the Cross.

---

[27] See D. M. MacKinnon, *Explorations in Theology* 5 (London, 1979), especially papers 5 and 11.

2
Explaining the
Non-Realist Theology

2

Faith Alone

ALTHOUGH THERE IS NOW SOME DISPUTE about its precise date
(1910, or 1913?), the abstract watercolor "Improvisation" by
Wassily Kandinsky has long been regarded as the first wholly
non-realist or non-representational painting in Western art. In
connection with this momentous event, Kandinsky himself
told the following story, dating the incident in the year 1908:

> It was twilight. I was returning immersed in thought from my
> sketching, when on opening the studio door I was suddenly
> confronted by a picture of indescribable and incandescent love-
> liness. Bewildered, I stopped, staring at it. The painting lacked
> all subject, depicted no identifiable object, and was entirely
> composed of bright color-patches. Finally I approached closer
> and only then recognized it for what it really was—my own
> painting standing on its side on the easel. The following day,
> by daylight, I tried to recapture the impression I had experi-
> enced the day before, but I could not do so entirely.

The story is a very good one, even though anyone habituated
to biblical criticism—and therefore having an evil, suspicious
mind—will smile and recognize that here is a tale that has
been told many times by a man intent on building up a myth.
The odd combination of twilight with incandescence and
bright color, and the equally dubious claim to *remember* a state
of being immersed in thought, show us that what Kandinsky
is doing is setting the scene for a moment of revelation. To
confirm this there is a doublet, for Kandinsky has a second
and earlier story of how he first saw a painting as an abstract.
It dates from 1895, when he saw one of Monet's "Haystacks"
series at an exhibition in Moscow:

"It was the catalogue that taught me that I was looking at a
haystack. I was incapable of recognizing it . . . I had confusedly
felt that an object was lacking in the painting."

Yet although Monet's work was almost non-figurative (and could be seen as being wholly so) it proved to be extraordinarily memorable: "at the most unexpected moments one saw it float before one's eyes with its slightest details." This story also has a religious flavor, for it leads to a vocation: Kandinsky used to tell it to explain why he had chosen to become a painter.

Like such contemporaries as Malevich and Mondrian, Kandinsky was articulate about the reasons why the move to non-realism had been made. Precedents had been found in the tradition, for example in those passages in paintings by Delacroix that had so impressed Seurat, passages which when viewed close-up dissolved into splashes and brief strokes of brilliant color. The rise of a new commercial and industrial middle-class society in which art no longer had its old public function had forced painting to become critically self-conscious. It turned back to examine itself and its own techniques, even though in so doing it perforce ran the risk of alienating and bewildering the public. It had to do so because the rise of mechanical ways of recording nature—science in general, and the camera in particular—had called into question the traditional assumption that a work of art gets its value and its justification from the way it signifies something else that stands beyond itself. Kandinsky saw German Idealist philosophy and, above all, music as suggesting the possibility of an alternative, non-mimetic and purely expressive artistic practice. He strove to create a form of painting in which, as he said in 1912, line would be "free of the obligation to designate a thing in a painting, and would itself function as a thing." The painting would no longer be a mere copy; it would be seen as standing alone, and not having to pretend any more to be anything other than itself.

Even more important to the first non-figurative painters was the revolution in physics, which seemed to show that a centuries-old construction of the world, going back to the Renaissance and the scientific revolution, was not after all constitutive of reality but had merely been imposed upon reality by the human mind. For centuries the painter's eye had looked upon something like a Newtonian world, with masses disposed in Euclidean space. The composition of a traditional painting, with its heavy "bottom," reflecting the earth's gravitational pull, with its up and down, left and right, with its framed and balanced vision, was based on a world-view that was no longer seen as being objective and compulsory, but as human and optional. Painting was now free to break out of that order. This is the significance of the "floating" of Monet's picture, and of the fact that Kandinsky's own painting lay on its side. A painting seen topside-up is locked into our normal cosmological vision; but when turned on its side and seen afresh, it is broken out of that vision and stands alone in a moment of revelation.

At first the break with realism and the move to a nonrepresentational art appeared to be a revolutionary change, as if all painting hitherto had suddenly been found to be worthless because it had rested on a mistaken theory. But this sense of discontinuity was only temporary. Many of the abstract artists themselves thought rather in terms of continuity, and in time art history was rewritten to demonstrate that continuity. What is more, not all art was instantly obliged to become abstract expressionist. Realism continued, and in later generations might be revived—though with the proviso that abstract art had made a permanent, and valuable, difference in the way we see all art. Neo-realism cannot be quite the same thing as realism was in the old days before the move to abstraction had been made.

By now the point to which this elaborate metaphor is leading must be becoming increasingly obvious to the reader, but one more detail may be added. Confronting abstract art, some people suspect that they may be the victims of a confidence trick. They feel that an art not humbled and disciplined by the task of representing an object truthfully must become arbitrary. It refuses to bow to objective standards by which it can be tested. It is egoistic, arrogant, self-indulgent, and insincere. To which it may be replied that the new kind of art is in practice found to impose very severe standards, and to demand purity of heart and motive more stringently than ever.

Where there is a sitter and a need to please him, there are many temptations to flattery, evasion, and deceit. But where the artist is alone, and his work is nothing but an expression of and a terrible judgement upon himself, the commitment to art required of him becomes unconditional. More than ever, there is something hidden to which he must be *true*, something that has the qualities of eternity, absoluteness, and inescapability about it.

We leave it at that, and suggest that religious thought today stands where painting stood in 1910 or so. It is becoming non-representational. A long history has brought us to the point where the representationalist model of what we are trying to do in our religious worship, faith, and practice no longer satisfies us. Resting as it does on a false and obsolete metaphysics, realist religion is bad religion in the same way as James Tissot's paintings are bad art, and a religious imperative drives us to challenge it. One factor in this has been the rise of a new kind of society in which religion does not have the same place as formerly, and the new self-criticism to which religious thought has therefore been led. Another has been the rise of powerful alternative methods of representing reality—in particular, science. But at a deeper level, there has been the realization, stemming from German Idealist philosophy, that all systems of representation, whether scientific or religious, are merely human conventions with a limited span of useful life; a realization that has undermined the very concept of representation itself. The very notion that either science or art or religion can get their justification from their simple accuracy in registering and responding to objective and independent structures "out there" has broken down.

The point we are making is general, applying equally to science, art, and religious belief. The idea of copying has broken down because we can never get into a position in which we can set the copy and the pure original side by side for comparison. We see many kinds of copy, but we never see any original just as it is, an objective mind-independent real structure, out there and independent of our systems of representation. We see things only in representation, and never absolutely. We can compare the way things look under different points of view or perspectives, but we do not have any absolute or perspectiveless vision of things that we can use as a standard for testing the accuracy of the various perspectival visions. Their justification must become simply pragmatic.

Nietzsche was a philosophical perspectivist, who suggested that every philosopher's system and vision of the world was a disguised and projected spiritual autobiography. The move to abstraction in painting reflected this idea, art becoming a creative expression of the artist's own subjectivity. In the process, the standards to which the artist had to work were internalized: what counted now was not the external accuracy of the copying-relation, but inner honesty, truthfulness, sincerity, and fidelity to his vocation as an artist. Art for art's sake, autonomous art, could be and was ridiculed as élitist and self-indulgent, and the same criticisms have been leveled more recently against the idea of the autonomy of religion. But many or most people are now ready to acknowledge that abstract art is real art, that it imposes its own very strict spiritual discipline, and that in any case we have now reached a point where we no longer feel the need to draw any sharp distinction between abstract and figurative works. We are ready to acknowledge that the inner imperatives to which the abstract artist found himself subject, and which he felt so powerfully, apply to all artists alike. Figurative and nonfigurative art are judged by the same standards.

That being conceded, then we may be ready to allow that abstract art has made a dent in the way we see all art, and to recognize why it is that music is at once the least figurative, the most purely expressive, and the closest to religion of all art forms. And now, after all this, we are free to revive various sorts of realism as the spirit moves us. But it will be realism *after* abstraction, realism with a difference. And so it is with religion.

There is one important point on which my analogy between religious thought and painting has already been challenged. Some say that the notion of an *avant-garde* is misleading. It is romantic and self-indulgent for a theologian to see himself as a trailblazer, the barometer of his age, in the travail of whose soul the future is born. On the contrary, the theologian does not and cannot lead the way. The church does indeed slowly evolve historically, but it does so under the guidance of the Spirit and it moves as a body; theologians as such are not called to be more than mere interpreters of processes already going on. The very notion of an *avant-garde* thinker or artist itself belongs to a rather brief historical period, and one that is past.

I agree with much of this. Most theologians are indeed quite properly commentators, interpreters, and historians. In their work as teachers they usually act as armorers, equipping the young soldiers whom the church is sending out into the field, rather than engaging in warfare themselves. If indeed we do stand at a time when a major shift in religious consciousness has to take place, there is no special reason why it should be theologians rather than any others who pioneer it.

Yet someone must; or so I believe. To judge by the pace of cultural change within the past thirty years, the church, if not renewed, will decline irreversibly into a marginal, enclosed "cult" within a lifetime from now. The religious life and the contemplative virtues could be lost. It is urgently necessary to demythologize Christian belief completely and to achieve conceptual and practical renewal, because if the task is not undertaken very soon it will be too late. At times I fear that it is too late already.

Some irrationalists argue that because superstitions flourish among the people at large, and look like continuing to do so, supernaturalist faith may also happily continue to be believed. They point to the prevalence of superstition and fundamentalism as evidence that nonrational belief has a rosy future ahead of it.

It probably does; but it is none of our concern. We are talking about true religion, which must be rigorously rationalist, and about the kind of change that is needed in order to save it.

The change is, at bottom, philosophical, and therefore raises difficult questions for the church. From early times

Christianity has been clothed in Greek metaphysics. This tradition in philosophy was strongly realist and cosmological, and was amalgamated with Christian theism by means of the idea of degrees of reality. Philosophy was essentially a quest for the knowledge of the truly real, and all the possible objects of knowledge were arranged on a rising scale of degrees of being. In Plato's analogy of the Line, fleeting images and sense-experiences were on the lowest rung of the ladder. Of them we could have no more than "illusions." The everyday world of physical objects came next and could be the object of "belief." Ascending the scale, one then crossed the line between the visible and the invisible worlds, and came to the realm of ideas: universal concepts, mathematical objects, moral essences. Of these objects one could have discursive knowledge. Finally, at the summit of the system stood the most-real Being of all and the object of pure rational intuition, the Form of the Good, or in Christian Platonism, God.

For Christian theism, God's mode of being was, of course, not directly knowable. Nevertheless, the idea of God's objective existence was given a sort of intelligibility by the idea of degrees of being. If one could say of any two objects whatever, "This has more reality than that," then one had the beginnings of a scale which, when extrapolated *ad infinitum*, would give the mode of God's eternal existence. And although it was in itself incomprehensible, that infinite degree of reality must be actual, because all the lower degrees had descended from it.

The whole metaphysics depended on the mythological idea that Being or Reality was a sort of stuff or a quality that could be present in varying degrees of intensity or concentration. What happened in the eighteenth century with Hume and Kant was not so much that the old arguments for the existence of God were discovered to be invalid, but rather that the idea of degrees of being broke down, and therefore the thinkability of God's objective existence was lost. The objects of natural science, mathematics, and morality could no longer be arranged on a neat linear scale. No ladder pointed up to heaven.

To say that something existed was merely to say that a concept could be applied.

This meant that there was now no mean between a purely ideal God and an idol. Either you had to think of God as existing in the same way as other things do, or you had to think of him as a pure guiding ideal.

For nearly two hundred years theology has been caught in this dilemma. Many of the dominant (and therefore supposedly "orthodox") schools of theology today have chosen to be an unhappy mixture of pantheism and sheer equivocation. On the one hand they follow Hegel in regarding God less as a distinct individual than as the inner Ground and still-to-be-completed evolving Totality of all things, and on the other they also seek to identify him with supreme Value. They therefore exude a vague and holistic cosmic optimism which is radically at odds with the tragic and fragmented character of modern experience, and which carries no conviction at all.

If the situation is as I have described it, the reasons why the revolt takes the form it does will be apparent. Radicals admire the earlier protests of Blake, of Kierkegaard against Hegel, and of dialectical theology against liberalism; but in particular they think it necessary finally to exorcise the ghost of the old realist metaphysics. The core of Christianity to be salvaged will be its ethics, its spirituality, and its "categories"—that is, a certain set of determinations of the spiritual life. Faith will be consistently post-metaphysical, active, creative, and autonomous in a barren universe. The divine imperative that constrains it, and gives to it its own kind of objectivity, will be very similar to the inner imperative earlier described as constraining an artist. To have faith in God will be to have a vocation; it will be to acknowledge the supreme authority of that requirement in the shaping of one's whole life. In this way there can be—and indeed there always was—a truly religious faith in God which is logically independent of realist metaphysics, and can still be maintained in a post-metaphysical world.

However, it is no secret that within the church there is not much enthusiasm for this idea. Many are baffled by it, and others consider that it can have no place within her walls, but should go out and live in the desert where it belongs. The alliance of Christian faith with realist metaphysics is so ancient that people find it impossible to imagine that faith can exist alone.

The churches indeed have a problem. They possess bodies of supernatural doctrine, articulated in creeds, conciliar definitions, and Reformation confessions of faith. Traditionally, the limits of permissible deviation were defined in simply theological terms. This was adequate, so long as the underlying Plato-and-Aristotle philosophical consensus more or less held and was not yet itself seriously in dispute. But when it broke own, and philosophy became fast changing and increasingly pluralistic, new problems arose. It became disconcertingly clear how much Christian doctrine had always depended upon its philosophical partner to give it meaning and make it fruitful. Now, philosophy rather than theology became the issue.

Some thought that a purely autonomous and yet objective theology, independent of philosophy, could be developed on the basis of the scriptural revelation alone. However, the last great attempt to establish theology as an autonomous science, made on a heroic scale by Karl Barth, is now widely thought to have failed. Without a philosophical explanation of the status of its language, without a philosophy to make connections between the language of Scripture and other areas of human language, Barth's vast narrative theology hangs in a kind of limbo. We do not know what to make of it.

One response to Barth's failure might be to give up the notion that theology can or should be a science, an articulated body of objective knowledge of divine things. Most people, however, are reluctant to accept this. Their conclusion is that in order to make theology a science, an alliance with philosophy is necessary. But which philosophy? On the market today may be found versions of Christianity inspired and given meaning and applicability by the philosophies of Aquinas, Kant, Hegel, Marx, Heidegger, Wittgenstein, Teilhard de Chardin, Whitehead, and many more.

This diversity is most uncomfortable, and raises many more questions than it answers. Each version of Christianity thus produced may pay lip-service to the old system of supernatural doctrines, but when several faith-and-philosophy alliances are before us for inspection we see how profoundly faith is transformed by her chosen philosophical bedfellow. How is the church to decide which philosophies are eligible partners? How does the pope know that Christianity can be married to Aristotle, or indeed (as in his own case) to Edmund Husserl and phenomenology, but may *not* contract an alliance with Marxism? The limits of permissible deviation here being laid down are not primarily theological but philosophical, and the drawing of limits in the philosophical realm is not easy for the churches. Where do they get their authority to do it, and where do they find their criteria? Such past experience as they have had does not furnish encouraging precedents. There have been cases, including that of Aristotelianism itself, where a philosophy was at first judged to be incompatible with Christianity, but then later there was a marked change of policy. Past experience suggests that in these matters first thoughts are often wrong.

Even worse, though, is the problem of the manifest dominance of the philosophical partner in every such alliance. The pope may feel that liberation theology is a wolf in sheep's clothing, not true Christianity but merely Marxism made palatable for a Catholic culture, Marxism dressed up in a Christian vocabulary. He may be right, but if he is, then we should add that the same might equally be said in the other cases also. Eastern Orthodoxy is a tuppence-colored version of neo-Platonism. Bultmann's theology is merely the atheistic existentialism of early Heidegger proclaimed from a pulpit in the language of Protestantism. Process theology continues the philosophical theology of the later William James in being a liberal Protestant version of the American Dream. Teilhard's theology is merely Julian Huxley's secular evolutionary religion with some religious labels stuck on it. And so on. We are suggesting that it looks as if the pope's criticisms of liberation theology are equally applicable to all other systems of thought in which Christian faith is married to a particular philosophy.

How has all this come about? The church's body of supernatural doctrines is ultimately derived from the strange mythological thought-world of late ancient Judaism. God was seen in somewhat anthropomorphic and highly interventionist terms. Human life was subject to frequent invasions from the heavenly world above and the infernal regions below. The conception of history was dispensationalist; that is, history was a drama in several acts, rapidly approaching its final *dénouement* when, amid supernatural convulsions, the present world-order would be terminated, the evil powers would be bound, the dead would be raised, and the Messiah's new world would come.

Such a world-view, untouched by science or philosophy and without any developed conception of a natural law-governed course of things, was as bizarre to the Greeks as it is to us. The Acts of the Apostles pictures Paul at Athens as having already been aware of the problem and endeavoring to sweeten his message with a tincture of Greek philosophy (Acts 17:16–32). This set the pattern for the future. The Gospel was to be made a universal faith by being amalgamated with Greek philosophy, which contributed ideas of reason, the soul, the cosmic order, the degrees of being, and so on. The old supernaturalism, witnessed to by Scripture, came to be set within the context of a larger and more regular cosmic vision, a philosophy of nature and God; and it was thereby given a realist interpretation, which was what the church wanted.

Because the synthesis worked fairly well for so long, it is not surprising that people should even today be still attempting to construct something of the same general type. From the Renaissance onwards, criticism developed both of the old supernatural faith and of the "scholastic" philosophy with which it was allied. But the criticism was itself commonly framed in terms of a broadly realist viewpoint, allowing the impression to persist that the old order might yet be reconstituted on the basis of an alliance between an appropriately liberalized and reinterpreted supernaturalism and an updated version of realist metaphysics. Hence all the modern thrashing about in search of the right philosophical marriage-partner for theology.

Our suggestion, however, is that old-style realist metaphysical systems are all of them alike obsolete. The lesson may be learned in different ways from American pragmatism, from the career of Wittgenstein, from the social sciences, or from the French philosophy of the past twenty years. Unaware of the nature of language and so not fully critical, old-style metaphysics is itself just as mythological as supernatural theology. It is impotent to perform for Christian theology the service that was expected of it in the past. So we have come to a new situation, and must seek to articulate Christian faith in a new way. For an autonomous and post-metaphysical world, a post-metaphysical or non-realist faith.

Those who are attempting to define such a faith can only plead for time and for toleration. The period of transition is inevitably difficult. Our discussion has suggested that in a normal period, when the general philosophical framework is holding, church authority may be in a position to fix, in advance, the boundaries of permissible theological deviation; but that in a period of deep change, when the real problems are philosophical, it is to say the least doubtful whether church authority can usefully attempt to define limits within which Christian thought must keep. In a time like ours, no pre-conditions can be laid down. Everything is negotiable. But when the time of transition is over, we may expect to see continuity restored.

3

Anti-Realist Faith

AROUND TWO HUNDRED YEARS AGO a change came over Western thought. It became much more aware of itself and of its own interpretative and constructive activity than it had been before. Slowly, thinking shifted from being dogmatic to being critical. A whole new realm came into view, as people became conscious of the hitherto hidden apparatus by which we put a construction upon our experience. At first, the rationalists and Kant tried to prove that there was nothing very alarming about the new discovery, because (they said) this thinking machinery of ours is timeless and necessary. They argued that the world *must* be thought in the way that it is thought, so that for these first critical thinkers reality still held firm. But later, as it became obvious that people do, in fact, see the world and think of the world very differently in different societies and historical periods, it came to be recognized that all our thinking is historically conditioned. Whereas the older dogmatic type of thinking had always tended to go straight from the mind to the cosmos, critical thinking became preoccupied with the variable cultural apparatus that guides the way we perceive and interpret what's out there.

Philosophy did not give up. As before, it fought a determined rearguard action in favor of necessary truth. Like Kant, Hegel also believed that the difference between science and philosophy is that science is concerned with what merely happens to be so, whereas philosophy is concerned with what must be so. Accordingly, he tried to prove that there remains a sort of rational necessity in the way that, living just where and when I do, I must perceive the world as I do. That is, Hegel tried to show that there is philosophical necessity in the process of historical development and in the succession of human cultural forms. As everyone knows, Karl Marx and other historicist thinkers held the same view; but eventually it broke down, leaving a doctrine which has been called perspectivism.

The main doctrines of perspectivism are as follows. There isn't any pure or quite neutral experience or knowledge of reality. In order to have any experience or knowledge at all, you must have a practical slant, an interest, an angle, or a perspective which, so to say, makes certain things stand out and become noticeable. To take the simplest possible example, acute hunger may give you an interest in dividing up the world in such a way that the edible stands out from its inedible background. There are indefinitely many such perspectives or angles upon the world—and they are all of them historically occasioned, human, and contingent. Some, like certain branches of our natural sciences, are very highly refined. But even the most advanced scientific theories are still human, perspectival, historically evolved, and subject to future revision. None of them can claim the sort of dogmatic absoluteness that people thought they had in pre-critical times, when all the most important knowledge was unchanging and came down to us from the past and from above.

So reality has now become a mere bunch of disparate and changing interpretations, a shifting loosely-held coalition of points of view in continual debate with each other. Politics is like that nowadays, and so is every faculty in a modern university. So is human reality generally, which is why in modern culture we represent reality to ourselves predominantly through an endless proliferation of perspectival fictions, in the novel, drama, and the cinema. We are all of us non-realists nowadays.

The position just described was reached by Nietzsche during the 1880s. He used the slogan, "There are no facts, only interpretations," and he coined the term "anti-realism" to describe his doctrine. At the same time, critical thinking was preparing to advance yet another stage as it became aware of language. The new development appeared in the United States in C. S. Peirce's doctrine of thought-signs, in Austria in Fritz Mauthner's philosophy of language, and in Switzer-

land in Ferdinand de Saussure's structural linguistics, but it
achieved really wide currency only as the work of Wittgenstein and the French structuralists became known in the
1950s.

Most of the key new ideas about language are by now very
familiar. People seem to start by thinking that language is a
more or less unsatisfactory dress in which we clothe our
thoughts, and that the meaning of a word is an object outside
language, as if a word is a label. Because we think there has to
be something for a word to stand for, we suppose that the
great words of philosophy, religion, ethics, and so forth must
stand for unchanging and invisible essences, like the Platonic
Ideas. Thus laws, standards, values, concepts, and the rest are
thought of as being rather like spirits, but impersonal; they are
seen as ghostly things that control events. So the popular view
of language makes us realists in philosophy and in theology.

The linguist's vision of language is, however, quite different. To him, it is a very large, historically evolving and living
system. In effect, it coincides with culture, seen as a system
of signs. There is no need to go outside language in order
to explain it. We are always already within language, and the
dictionary is well able to explain every printed mark simply in
terms of its relations with other printed marks. A word's meaning cannot be anything external to language because any and
every meaning is just a presently held position within a vast
dynamic and evolving system of relativities. Since there cannot be any unchanging meaning, there cannot be any timeless
truths. The whole world of meaning, which is the true starting
point for philosophy, is by its very nature shifting all the time
like the prices in a stock market, as human power relations
shift.

Like the prices in a stock market, the meanings of words
are essentially publicly determined, for a meaning is the resul-
tant of an interplay of forces in the public domain. The philosophers who first saw this, such as C. S. Peirce, quickly grasped
that it meant the end of the individualistic approach to philosophy that had dominated the West since the Reformers and
Descartes. I cannot determine any meanings all by myself, so

I cannot begin my philosophy from myself. Society and the public domain come first. Culture is a system of symbols, and society is a busy communications network. Messages in the various codes are flying back and forth all the time, and we all contribute to the humming activity of the whole.

Concerning the meanings of the symbols used in society's communication code, there is an amazingly high level of agreement. Each one of us is phenomenally sensitive to just what is and is not currently being done with each individual word in present-day idiomatic English, and we are all the time minutely adjusting our own usage in response to social change and new things that we've heard being said. Our desire for mutual understanding and sympathy must be very strong for it to have produced such a refined unanimity as there is among any local group of native speakers on their own home ground.

The comparison that I am drawing between our continual public debate about everything and a market brings out a striking difference between meaning and truth. On the one hand, through our ceaseless chatter we achieve a very high degree of consensus about the meanings of words. On the other hand, in our modern large-scale and highly communicative societies, there is no single grand overarching dogmatic truth any longer. All truths, beliefs, theories, faiths, perspectives become just individual stocks in the market. They rise and fall relative to each other as conditions change.

Now comes the point that is hard to grasp: just as there is no sense in asking for the absolute price of something, so there is no sense in trying to step outside the changing human debate and fix realities, meanings, and truths absolutely. We have to live and act without absolutes. To take just one example, I personally am prepared to fight tooth and nail for modern evolutionary biology against creationism. But I cannot claim that current evolutionary theory is, in any part of it, objectively, dogmatically, and perennially just true. On the contrary, over the generations to come I expect that every bit of current evolutionary theory will be replaced by something different. In this shifting relativistic world of ours, we can still choose our values and fight for them, but our beliefs won't have the old kind of permanent anchorage in an unchanging ideal order.

The point here is hard to express without paradox, but let's try: our modern experience is that there isn't any objective, fixed, intelligible reality out there, such as may be replicated in our language and invoked to check our theories. We now live wholly *inside* our own history, our language, and the flux of cultural change. We find that our world isn't made of Being any more, but of symbols and of conflicting arguments. The long-term effect of the critical revolution in our thinking has been to make us so much aware of our own theories, viewpoints, and ways of thinking that objective reality has melted away. We haven't got a proper cosmos any longer, only a bunch of chronic disagreements.

Let us now, by contrast, briefly evoke the traditional religious and philosophical outlook of medieval Christianity. It was Platonic, making a sharp contrast between this changing and corruptible material world below and the eternal controlling intelligible world above. It was pre-critical, so that people made no very clear distinction between culture and nature. They blithely supposed that their own cultural conceptions were part of the natural order of things. It was pre-scientific, so that many events were ascribed to supernatural causes. It was also pre-historical, so people's vision of the past was short and very hazy. Life was governed by tradition, a fixed body of knowledge that had come down from the Fathers and from above. Faith was therefore dogmatic; binding you to a body of truths and a form of life that would remain immutable from the primitive era until the end of historical time.

In such a context, both philosophy and theology were oriented toward necessity, changelessness, and ideal perfection. For both traditions the goal of human life was to attain absolute knowledge of absolute reality. In that timeless contemplation of absolute necessity and perfection, which religion called the Vision of God, you would find perfect fulfillment and happiness. Thus the old Christian culture was highly realistic in being centered around objective, eternal, necessary, intelligible, and perfect Being. Faith was dogma-guided longing for Heaven, and the monk whose way of life anticipated Heaven was the highest human type. The body, time, culture, language, disagreement, history, and biological life were all relatively neglected or disparaged.

Now consider how completely we have reversed the traditional outlook of Christian Platonism. The world above and all the absolutes are gone. The whole of our life and all our standards are now inside language and culture. For good or ill, *we* make our own history, *we* shape our own world, *we* together evolve all norms to which our life is subject. Religion for us must inevitably be something very different from what it was in the heyday of Platonic realism. Indeed, it is plain that if I am right, then Christianity must be revolutionized to survive.

There are people who still hope that the old order can be restored. For them, there is no intermediate position; the end of dogmatism is the beginning of nihilism. They are terrified by the thought of a world without certainties. They yearn for a society constrained by one absolute truth determined by one absolute power. But anti-realists like me reject their view and claim that Christianity can and should be modernized. We invoke the symbol of the Day of Pentecost, when God scattered Himself and was distributed as spirit to each individual believer. Just as Truth has come down from heaven and is now immanent within the movement of our various human conversations; just as political sovereignty is no longer wholly vested in a superperson above society but is dispersed throughout the body politic; just as, indeed, the whole of the former world above is now resolved down into the life of this world—so God also is now in each of us.

This discussion has, I hope, made a little clearer what we mean by a non-realist philosophy of religion. Realists think our religious language tells of beings, events, and forces that belong to a higher world, an invisible second world beyond this world of ours. But I believe that there is only one world and it is this world, the world we made, the human life-world, the world of language. To think of language as replicating the structure of some extra-linguistic reality, some world beyond the world of our language, is, I believe, a mistaken way of thinking of language *anyway*. Every word is more like a tool for doing a job than like a photocopy of something that is not a word. The only language we can know is wholly human, completely adapted to its job of being the medium in which human life is lived in the only world we have. So we should see religious language in terms of the part it can play in our lives, rather than see it in a mythological way as conjuring up a picture of a second world. For us, there is only *one* world, and it is *this* world, the manifest world, the world of language, the world of everyday life, of politics and economics. And this world has no outside. It doesn't depend in any way on anything higher, and there is no meaning in the suggestion that our cultural beliefs and practices need to be set on any external foundation.

Thus I believe in only one continuous but multi-perspectival common world. In it language and experience, meaning and feeling, nature and culture are fully interwoven. This one world is human, cultural, and historically changing. Religion is wholly inside it, and it has no outside. I don't take a realistic view of *any* non-manifest entity. The Word has become flesh, say Christians: that is, the intelligible world must now be resolved back into its manifest basis.

This fully secularized and incarnational vision of things became dominant about two centuries ago. Among the historical events that marked its emergence were the industrial revolution, the democratic revolutions, the romantic movement, German Idealist philosophy, and the rise of the novel. It is emergent in David Hume, but is stated most grandiosely by Hegel. More recently its implications have been spelt out in one way by American pragmatists like Richard Rorty, who follow John Dewey, and in another way by Nietzsche and the modern French philosophers who admire him.

These may seem a disparate group of thinkers, but what they have in common is a desire to escape from the legacy of Plato. They are all naturalistic. They reject two-worlds dualism, and, in particular, they see our life as being so profoundly historical that there can be no sense in the idea that we are subject to the controlling influence of a timeless order. Our language, our knowledge, and our morality are human and ever-changing, not cosmic. There's no point in trying to assess them in terms of their relation to just one set of timeless, superhuman intellectual and moral standards.

An example: conservatives sometimes complain that moral or academic standards are lower than they used to be. But the world of two or three generations ago was a different world, with different standards. In their world, they measured things by their standards; in our world we measure them by ours. We have no more reason to absolutize their standards than we have to absolutize our own. In fact, we shouldn't absolutize *either* set of standards: instead we should simply recognize that historical change happens and that it demands a continuous reinterpreting and recreating of our standards.

In this way we come to see that our standards and all our supposed "absolutes" are themselves historical, immanent within language and subject to continual remaking. This has, in turn, the effect of making certain old ways of thinking no longer possible to us. Consider for example "the Word of God." Our understanding of what language is has become so fully human, cultural, and historical that we now cannot conceive a solitary non-human and extra-historical language user. At one time people naively saw God as a member of their own language group. He spoke to them in the tongue of their own place and time. But how shall we put it now? To what language community does God belong? In what dialect and of what period is God's speech, and how in terms of modern linguistic theory do His words have meaning for Him? What instinctual drives power His utterance, and what body has He to vibrate as He produces it?

Just to raise these questions is to realize that a realistic view of God as a language user has long been impossible to us. And as we turn now to the philosophy of religion, I must repeat that I am merely describing the world as it has been these past two centuries. It is the world as ordinary people experience it in their political and economic life, and represent it to themselves in the novel, the newspapers, and the cinema. It is the way the world is for students of language, the social sciences, and history. I cannot say that it is the metaphysical truth of the human condition, because it is how things look after the end of metaphysical truth. No one vision of things can any longer be compulsory. The philosopher cannot claim the authority to act as culture-policeman. Instead, he'll have to be something more like an interpreter of the times, who seeks to show *both* the diversity of the possibilities at present before us *and* the family resemblance among all the perspectives and forms of life that are available in some one period, such as our own. So I am not telling you how things are absolutely, but only offering you an interpretation of the way they seem, just now.

It is in that undogmatic and post-authoritarian spirit that we return to the question of realism and anti-realism in the philosophy of religion.

First, we must obviously acknowledge that the majority report of tradition comes down in favor of theological realism. Most believers have thought that supernatural beings and influences really exist, independently of us. They have thought that there is a real God out there controlling world events, who may intervene, assist us by His Grace, answer our prayers, and so on; and they have thought that there is a real supernatural world wherein we may go on living after we have died. That surely is how most people have seen matters.

There are, however, two massive exceptions to this generalization. First, the ancient tradition of Christian Platonism clearly recognized that our words are only human words, and accordingly stressed the descriptive inadequacy of all our talk about divine things so strongly as to be agnostic. Between the third century and the Reformation, most of the great theologians stood in this tradition. Secondly, the Hebraic and Protestant tradition always saw religious language as being imperative rather than indicative. It tells us how we must think and live, rather than how things are. Its purpose is to govern rather than to inform. These two themes, the negative theology and voluntarism, have between them ensured that throughout the Christian tradition, the intellectuals have been much less realistic in their belief than ordinary people.

This has continued to be true in the modern period. The great founders of modern religious thought, Kant, Hegel, and Schleiermacher, were all in their different ways anti-realists about God, two centuries ago. Their influence has ensured that most of the long line of Continental theologians since have been anti-realists also, but they used slightly veiled language and their English readers have not understood what has been happening. This was true, for example, of Schweitzer, Bultmann, Neibuhr, Bonhoeffer, and Tillich in our own century. The case of church history is also very notable, for fully non-supernaturalist church history began to be written in the Prussian universities in the 1740s, and nobody today complains that it leaves out anything. We seem to accept that purely secular church history tells the whole story.

Furthermore, we habitually put forward an anti-realist interpretation of *other people's* religious beliefs. Thus, I have at home several small bronze images of Shiva. Ask me, and I can, in principle if not in fact, tell you all there is to know about Shiva and how he is worshipped, and I don't have to leave anything out. I need miss nothing, I can sympathetically explain everything, and I can even join in if I wish. The anti-realism consists in the recognition that Shiva is real only to his followers and within their perspective. If Hinduism vanished from the earth, there'd be nobody left to whom Shiva was real. But, for the present, Shiva lives. The anti-realist can, in principle, see all there is to see and say all there is to say. Since we have given up ideas of absolute truth and error, we can look down other perspectives without prejudice.

The anti-realist viewpoint has already made it possible for us to view other people's faiths more sympathetically, and to enter into them more deeply, than in the past. How much more then will we profit if we move over to an anti-realist view of *our own* faith!

The reason why we would gain so much is that realism in religion acts as an ideological defense of the *status quo*. It discourages us from attempting to carry through much needed reforms, and even prevents us from seeing their necessity. By suggesting that our religious beliefs were revealed to us by an

eternal and objective God, realism makes us afraid to question
them. And realism brings with it two other ideas that also in-
hibit us from thinking. *Essentialism* suggests that Christianity
is a timeless, coherent system of thought no part of which
can be altered without weakening the whole, and *primitivism*
maintains that faith was purest near its point of origin so that
we have to keep going back to the past for correction and for
legitimization.

All these ideas are surely wrong. To the historian's eye,
Christianity is not a timeless and coherent system of thought,
but a product of history and in continual change. It is a rather
loose aggregate or miscellany of ideas from different times and
places, many of which are at odds with each other. There is
no reason to think that just being old makes an idea more
likely to be right. On the contrary, we usually find that very
old ideas are now very bad, and need to be replaced. And
since critical study shows that, despite the myth of immutable
truth, Christianity has in fact been evolving throughout its
long history, there is no reason why we should not now do
openly and consciously what our forerunners did unknow-
ingly.

So, indeed, we *are* now doing, for we are increasingly aware
of our responsibility for modernizing Christianity and getting
it up to date. We set about bending the tradition and rewriting
history. We seek to purge the cruelty and sexism from Christian symbolism, and we begin to ordain women. By doing all
this we now admit that it was we who made our religious beliefs, it is we who are responsible for them, and it is up to us
to put them right. In short, our religious beliefs and practices
are an integral part of the evolving totality of culture, and must
change with it. So we acknowledge that religion is human,
historical, and cultural all the way through. It could not have
been otherwise. Nor does this matter, because if we remember our Bibles we'll recall that the religious system was never
intended to be an end in itself. It is only a means: eventually it
should make itself redundant, because the goal of the religious life is a spiritual state that is beyond all the symbols. So
you have to have the ladder to climb, and you have to know

when to kick it away. Often, religion fails to liberate people spiritually because they take its teachings too literally and don't know when and how to pass beyond them. In Asian religion it was a well-accepted principle that a particular name of God, or a particular set of worship-guiding images, should be used only for so long as they are helpful, and should then be left behind. People were encouraged to treat their own religious ideas lightly. In the West, unfortunately, our religious outlook has usually been heavy, crude, gloomy, and terroristic. The anti-realist point of view offers the prospect of Western religion becoming a little more sophisticated than it has been in the past. It's about time this happened, because Christianity as we have known it so far has been, frankly, barbarous compared with what it should be. We have been locked into truly frightful excesses of power and guilt, cruelty and sentimentality. We need a clean-up urgently.

Again, anti-realism helps, because now, for the first time, the believer no longer claims any special cosmic privilege. I am a priest, I practice Christianity in full, and I try to tread the spiritual path. I have found joy in loss, for now there is no remaining respect in which I think that I am in the light and some other human being is in darkness. I have no old-style supernatural or Plato-type metaphysical beliefs. I am as ignorant as everyone else, and I shall die like everyone else. Having no cosmic advantage, I can claim no spiritual authority or power over other human beings, and I have no moral standing for making them feel guilty. As I follow Christ I am now as naked as he is. By the standards of earlier centuries, my views are certainly radically skeptical. God is a guiding spiritual ideal; eternal life is holiness now. We must become radically emptied out and free. And in this state we can learn to practice Christianity a great deal better than in the past. The end of theological realism will at last make possible a Christian ethic that is more than mere obedience, an ethic of productive, world-changing, and value-realizing Christian action.

We can thus become creative for the first time in Christian history. In the old scheme of things, God did all the creating. God stood on the far side of the world; everything was ready-made for us and nothing much could be altered. Human beings were not in fact spoken of as creative before the eighteenth century. Today, by contrast, human creativity confronts the flux. God has moved round to our side and looks through our eyes. Christian action is now at last liberated. The believer is like an artist. The material we have to work on is our world and our own lives.

4

Free Christianity

CHRISTIAN NON-REALISM is the first fully critical and entirely non-dogmatic style of religious thought to appear in the West. It has been around for some years now, and has even developed into something of a movement, both in Britain and overseas, and both within and on the outer fringes of the churches. It has arisen out of the way modern philosophy has developed since Kant, and out of the way theology has been developing since Rudolf Bultmann and the debate about demythologizing the Gospel. There are places overseas, such as the Harvard Divinity School, where a version of it is even considered respectable. Furthermore, there are parallels to it in other communities, such as Mordecai Kaplan's Jewish reconstructionism, and American Jewish humanism. Yet, in spite of all this evidence for its "normality," non-realism makes only slow progress in Britain, and opposition to it remains fierce.

Why? Because there is a feeling that it has breached the final citadel. During the past century or so, theologians have demythologized almost the whole cycle of Christian supernatural doctrine. In approximate ascending order of gravity, the main items are the virginal conception of Jesus, miracles in general, the bodily ascension of Christ, the bodily resurrection of Christ, life after death, the divinity of Christ and even (rather recently) God's absolute foreknowledge, and God's personality. All these doctrines, it seems, can be questioned, and perhaps reinterpreted in a non-realistic sense. If Christ is your Lord and comes first in your life, you may believe him ascended without thinking that he shot up in the air, and if you experience a new and risen sort of life in Christ, you may believe him risen without necessarily having to think that once upon a time his corpse was galvanized back to life just like Frankenstein's monster. But God's objective existence is another matter. Non-realistic theists preserve all that is of specifically *religious* value in the idea of God. God, they say, is a guiding spiritual ideal, a symbol of the ultimate unity of our values, and a focus of spiritual aspiration. But (they continue) we cannot give any coherent account of God as a supposed objectively-existing being, and we cannot prove God's existence. We have only this life, and only our human language about God, to go on. We are not and will never be in a position to compare our talk of God with God absolutely, to see if the description is accurate. So we should give up the old metaphysical dogmas completely, remembering that we have no absolute knowledge. All our knowledge is only human knowledge, fallible and limited by language. Religion is simply a lot of stories and symbols, values and practices, out of which you must now evolve your own religious life. Think of yourself not as a soldier, but as an artist who has chosen to work mainly within a particular tradition. That is faith, the production of one's own life as a work of religious art.

The sense of spiritual liberation that we feel when we grasp all this is astounding. Why the fury?

The main difficulty is that for many centuries, religion has been seen as creed and faith as intellectual submission. The believer assents to a set of supernatural doctrines, doctrines that are above reason but which are certified to us by the authority of the Bible and the church—behind which of course stands the authority of God.

One philosophical doctrine is needed to support the whole system: metaphysical realism. No, it's not just a language-game, and it's not just poetry; it is considered vital to maintain the power of human language to jump right out of our everyday human world and express at least some true assertions about things transcendent and divine. Church leaders and fundamentalists alike are always "objectivists," in the sense that they perceive very clearly that their supernatural beliefs have no chance of being true or even meaningful, unless metaphysical realism is true. Hence the striking fact that orthodoxy now perceives the essence of Christianity not as anything religious—in *that* department we non-realists do much better than our critics—but as a philosophical doctrine, realism.

Unfortunately, metaphysical realism was permanently demolished by Kant, who went on to develop the first interesting modern non-realist account of God. In Britain we have been slow to understand what is going on, partly because our philosophers were mostly raised on Plato and Aristotle and not on Kant and Hegel, and partly because at the beginning of the twentieth century, Russell and Moore led the Anglo-Saxon world astray for generations by reintroducing a bizarre form of neo-realism (in Russell's case a realism of sense-data, and in Moore's even a naive realism about physical objects and our moral intuitions). But since the 1960s, the tide has turned with a vengeance; and I am not talking only of linguistic philosophy, but of linguistics, of psychology, and of the wholesale "naturalizing of epistemology" that is now going on. The intellectual future is thoroughgoing naturalism. Metaphysical realism may still have a few surviving defenders in the older generation, but the young know that it is dead, even in the Anglo-Saxon world. Today, Christian non-realism offers the churches their last chance of a rational future (though so far all the signs are that they will prefer the alternative, which is fundamentalism, on the grounds that it will offer them a much, *much* bigger market).

Christian non-realism, then, is thoroughly naturalistic in outlook, seeing the whole system of supernatural doctrine as poetry to live by—or, as Wittgenstein put it, "rules of life dressed up in pictures." In Britain it can be traced back to Matthew Arnold in the nineteenth century, and more recently to the so-called "non-cognitivism" of Richard Braithwaite and Richard Hare in the post-war years. I first described God as "non-objective" in 1979, coined the phrase "theological realism" in 1980, and introduced the term "non-realism" in 1982. I thought I was inventing it, but I now find that Hilary Putnam had already used it in the late 1970s. Putnam is a major American philosopher of the analytical school. From 1975 he was finding very strong reasons for rejecting realism, but he didn't want to go back to realism's traditional alternative, idealism.

So he used the term "non-realism." It is a cautious term, consciously undogmatic, which not only describes Wittgenstein's position accurately, but can be used to embrace almost all the leading schools of modern philosophy. The Americans talk about neo-pragmatism and post-analytical philosophy, the British talk about anti-realism and constructivism, and modern European philosophy has been well labeled "superstructuralism;" but what is common to all these various movements is a reaction against a certain conception of the philosopher's task. Philosophers were supposed to justify knowledge, which meant justifying the objectivity of knowledge, which meant justifying realism. Even people like A. J. Ayer, Bernard Williams, and Thomas Nagel have still felt that objective knowledge would be a good thing, and that realism does indeed occupy the high ground. It is what the philosopher should aspire after. But I'm using the term non-realism to embrace a wide variety of recent philosophical movements that want to get right away from those assumptions.

I'm saying, then, that I decline to be told that it's my job to justify knowledge, which means to prove its objectivity, which means to prove realism. And *that* is what I mean by non-realism—the refusal of a certain conception of the philosopher's task. I don't want to show how our knowledge copies an objective world; I only want to show what kind of a world our language gives us.

Let us spell out the contrast here in a little more detail. The difference between a realist and a non-realist is that a realist is a person who thinks that we have obviously got a ready-made world all laid on for us, whereas a non-realist is a person who says: "Hang on. How could we ever know that? Surely we humans are always inside our own historically evolved vision of the world? Over the millennia we've slowly built up our own conventions, our own languages, our own knowledge, our own beliefs and values. This human cultural superstructure that we've laboriously developed is all of a piece, all our own; and our relationship with it is two-way. We made it, we use it to make our world—and it makes us, too. Man is the cultural animal, as Aristotle should have said. Culture is a system of conventional signs in motion, and by trading them back and forth we build our public world. So how are we ever going to learn that the world our culture opens up to us goes on beyond the limits to which we ourselves have pushed it? Surely, so far as we are concerned, all meanings are meanings of bits of our language, all truths are statements true in our language, and all values are humanly-posited values. We are the only makers of all these things, aren't we? Meaning and truth exist only where *we* have constituted them. So how can we imagine ourselves learning that they were somehow *pre-existent*, ready-made and waiting for us out there before we human beings came along and started to discover them?"

In this opening statement the non-realist is saying that while our human cultural forms—our language, our theories, and so on—do indeed give us access to a world, the world they open up to us is inevitably just a humanly-constituted world. (Perhaps I should recall here that "world" is *wer-ald*, the age of a man.) It is *our* world, but it cannot be *the* world. The realist nevertheless still says that we do have a fully-determinate world, a real mind-independent cosmos, already laid on for us, and with a single moral order built into it. The non-realist may claim that scientists *invent* the laws of nature; but the realist intends to go on saying that scientists are progressively *discovering* the laws of nature. The non-realist says that we must invent new moral guidelines to cover problems thrown up by developments in reproductive medicine; but the realist says that all questions of right and wrong have objective answers, anticipated and determined in the mind of God from all eternity. The realist refuses to admit that there are problems about language, because in the realist view, the maker of the physical world and the maker of the moral order is also *our* maker, and he himself used language to build the world. The adequacy of language to copy the shape of reality is thus theologically guaranteed, and this brings us to the very heart of the realist case: the realist believes in a pre-established harmony between the structure of our language and the structure of reality, between thought and being, and between our moral constitution and the objective moral order of the world. In the realist view, the world was expressly made to be a home for us and a school of moral training, and we were made to fit into this home that God has set up for us. So there is no problem about language or about the objectivity of morality: the realist's belief in an objective metaphysical God is profoundly tied up with an optimistic and very homely cosmology. The old cosmologies were invented precisely in order to familiarize the terrible and cheer us up. That's why we have clung to them for so long: what really counts is not the evidence for them (it's nil) but our need of them.

Here then we come upon the region of sharpest conflict, because I can scarcely avoid the obvious corollary of the argument so far: a realist is a person who thinks that God made us and has himself taught us all we know about him, whereas a non-realist is a person who thinks we humans have ourselves developed all our ideas about our gods as *bonnes à penser*, and there's no way we could ever jump outside our own language and check whether our ideas about our gods correspond to the objective theological facts or not.

Indeed—and applying the present argument to the case of God—I'm arguing that from the non-realist point of view it is simply not the theologian's job to prove the objective existence of God, or even to ask what God is, but rather simply to ask what jobs the word "God" does now, and in what ways we can use it in building our world and our lives. For the non-realist, God's world-building and our own coincide. In the narrative theology of the Bible and Christian doctrine, talk about God helps us to debate and to battle with the great questions of the coherence of our values, the unity of all value, and the struggle between good and evil. But we are not talking metaphysics here, for these are human debates about human values, conducted within the conventions of a long-established literary genre. And, at a certain level, everybody is well aware that that is how it is.

A non-realist, then, thinks it obvious that we ourselves gradually evolved our own world-picture, our morality, and our religions; whereas a realist cordially dislikes "humanism" and "relativism" and insists that we owe everything to an objec-

tive God, who has himself settled all questions of truth and
value from all eternity, before ever we were created. God has
all the answers, and is indeed himself the whole Answer. In
religion and morality a realist will tend to be a traditionalist,
and probably also a revelationist. Religious authorities will
also have to endorse realism because it sees Truth as objective
and unchanging, and gives them clear credentials. They need
it; therefore it is true—for them, at least.

So realists think we live in a ready-made and stable world,
a divinely-created world of reassuringly authoritative and unchanging meanings, truths, and values, whereas non-realists
think that we live in a humanly-evolved world, *our* world, a
world in which all meanings, truths, and values depend on the
current state of the (human) argument. Non-realism is like
cosmic democracy: everything is seen as depending upon open
debate, healthy institutions, and a human consensus refreshed
by frequent injections of new metaphors, new valuations, new
angles. If the price of liberty is eternal vigilance, the price of
truth is endless openness to criticism and innovation. For the
realist, what makes the Truth obviously true is its preservation
unchanged; for the non-realist, what keeps truth true is the
vividness with which it is re-imagined and re-expressed.

This new conception of truth as being everywhere only-
human, democratic, and lower-case sharply divides realists
from non-realists. Will the religions remain locked into realism? If so, their future is already clear: it is fundamentalism.
Alternatively, what new forms might religious thought take in
response to the "end of metaphysics" and the coming of the
new post-realist world?

To see this question clearly, we need to kick away the ladder that we have just climbed. In order to state the argument
so far, I have made a contrast between *our world* and *the world*.
Our world is the world as we know it. Because all thought and
communication are transacted in cultural signs, our world is
always already a human world, coded into language, highly
interpreted and therefore a world that we ourselves have built.
We have contrasted our world, thus understood, with *the world*,
the world that according to realism exists independently of

our reading of it. And I seem to have argued that only *our world* exists; there is no *the world*. However, if my argument is valid the initial contrast between *our world* and *the world* must have been meaningless, and should not have been made. Our world being radically outsideless, there is no sense in the suggestion that there could be something else to contrast it with. So there has been a certain reflexive difficulty in the argument so far, and that is why it is now necessary to kick away the ladder. As soon as we have managed to reach the new point of view, we should immediately say to ourselves "But it is outsideless!," and we should forget the false and misleading contrast that was earlier made in order to help us get to this point. We haven't lost anything: everything is still *there*. But a deep philosophical shift has taken place.

Modern philosophy confuses us by using so many different vocabularies to describe the shift. "We are always inside . . ." Inside what? "Our own experience," say the empiricists; "The mind," say the idealists; "Our own humanity and our practical needs," say the pragmatists; "Language," or "the flux of signs," say the modern linguistic philosophers and superstructuralists.

In very recent years, I have perhaps added to the problem. I have been trying to restart philosophy, and get over the difficulty about reflexivity, by saying aloud: "We do best to picture the world at large as a beginningless, endless, and outsideless stream of language-formed events that continually pours forth and passes away—and this noise you hear is a typical bit of it."

In developing this vision of the world I try to abolish the traditional contrasts between language and reality, between subjectivity and objectivity, between matter and mind, and between the merely-human and the supernatural or divine. The aim is to produce an effect of complete happiness on the basis of thoroughgoing religious naturalism and world-affirmation. I use the label "energetic Spinozism" for this outlook, coupling it with what I call a "poetical theology" and a "solar (that is, expressivist) ethics."

Such is one form that religious thought may take in our

strange new world. Whereas the old medieval Christian universe (to which the churches are still committed) was very highly differentiated both vertically in space and horizontally in time, and elaborately scaled in degrees of being, rank, and value, we try to undo the old distinctions and concertina everything down into the outpouring present. The result is (or, at least, is intended to be) an effect of burning intensity. In the late 1980s, I used the term "active non-realism" for it: religion is no longer a theory of the world, but a practice of living, an art-like world-building activity. Now I prefer the term "solar ethics," the sun being an object whose living and dying are one and the same. Kierkegaard, expounding the Sermon on the Mount, speaks of living eternally in the present moment, and of regaining immediacy after reflection. When along these lines we undo the traditional binary oppositions and live in a way that fully unifies dying and living, time and eternity, the particular and the universal, immediacy and reflection, then human life and divine life have become each other. As that best of modern Christian writers, Nietzsche, puts it, "It is not a 'belief' which distinguishes the Christian: the Christian acts, he is distinguished by a *different* mode of acting . . . *evangelic practice alone* leads to God, it *is* God!" (*The Anti-Christ*, § 33).

All this may help to explain the much-criticized "belieflessness" of Christian non-realism. The non-realist Christian is a postmodern person who has lost all the old beliefs about finding the perfect, normative world elsewhere, either in the past, or in the world above, or in the future. The job of dogma was always to give us authoritative assurances that this present unsatisfactory world is only appearance: elsewhere there is a Real world that is free from all the limitations and miseries of this world.

The non-realist is a person who does not accept the old two-worlds doctrine, and therefore does not need dogmatic belief. There is only one world, the world that we have built up around ourselves, the world produced by our language. And non-realists argue that there is a practice of living by which we can find complete happiness in the here and now. Call it solar ethics, call it Love, call it eternal life.

So far in this discussion we have been sketching the philosophical and cultural context of Christian non-realism. We have limited ourselves to the West, but we should not leave this topic before noting that Mahayana Buddhism preserves a very rich tradition of non-realist philosophical and religious thought. Hence its great attractiveness to many younger Westerners today.

We turn now to consider briefly the *religious* context of non-realism, again limiting ourselves to the West. Let us begin from a feature of contemporary Anglo-Saxon societies—the mania for "political correctness," and "soundness;" the mania for sniffing out precisely where other people stand doctrinally and judging them accordingly. It is, of course, a legacy of Protestant doctrinal obsessions in particular, and more generally of the very long-standing use in our tradition of religious belief-systems as tools of social control. Our many creeds and confessions have usually appealed to the Bible for support.

Against this background, we begin by pointing out that the whole Bible, both Old and New Testaments, was written by Jews and that the Jews will themselves tell you that their faith is a practice-religion rather than a belief-religion. The contents and the literary forms of the biblical writings are so varied that although the Rabbis did develop a system of Jewish religious Law out of the Bible, they did not similarly develop a system of orthodox religious doctrine. In any case, the Jews are so literary that the very idea that language can be used precisely to define and enforce religious truth is foreign to them.

Against this background, one can see why non-realists like Kant and Wittgenstein tell us to see religious truth as being "regulative." Its function is not to give us metaphysical information, but to shape the way we live. Non-realists, looking again to our Jewish origins, want to see practice preceding theory and the lived religious life coming before the holding of sound doctrines.

Religious thought in the Hebrew Bible is for the most part

poetical and pre-philosophical, but here and there it does approach the philosophical style. This happens especially in Isaiah, chapters 40–55, where the writer reminds us a little of his contemporaries, the first Greek philosophers. The themes are similar, because he is ridiculing idolatry, thinking cosmologically, and insisting on the descriptive inadequacy of human language in speaking of God.

Here we see that modern non-realism represents the return in the critical period (the period since 1781, the date of Kant's first *Critique)* of very ancient themes in the Judeo-Christian tradition. In its first two centuries or so, Christian preaching to the Greco-Roman world always began with an attack on idolatry, and thereafter for another millennium it was intellectually dominated by the Negative Theology. Christianity was a way rather than a set of correct doctrines, and theology was not a university subject but rather guidance along the Way. You progressed by losing false and illusory beliefs, rather than by acquiring correct ones. In the Christian-Platonic mystical tradition the movement into God was a movement into Darkness and Nothingness, so that Christian spirituality could come to look and to sound surprisingly like the (non-theistic) spirituality of Buddhism; and it was strongly emphasized that the only human form under which God could be thought or represented was the human form of Christ. That is why Christ came to be portrayed as a cosmic, bearded figure: there was this Man, and behind him the dazzling darkness. That was all. Beautiful.

Modern Christian non-realists thus find much to admire in the old faith as it was until about A.D. 1200. But then things began to go very wrong. Aristotle's thought suddenly became a great influence upon theology. It is very much more realistic than Plato's, and Aristotle's conception of metaphysics as the science of being led to a steadily worsening objectification of God. Theology became a science studied in the universities, and the church became more and more a self-obsessed power-structure.

The preoccupation with power and hierarchy gradually displaced the old religion. Consider the way the crucifixion of

Jesus was treated in the later Middle Ages. In major ecclesiastical buildings, it became a symbol of the necessary submission of even the king to the pope. Christ, still a mature bearded man wearing the imperial crown, was crucified against the knees of the Father, who wore the papal tiara.

To a non-realist the crucifixion symbolizes the Negative Theology. Everything is made of signs, and all signs are fleeting. Everything must in the end be given up, even our very selves, even our idea of God. The crucifixion is an awesomely nihilistic image of the absolute nothingness from which we sprang, over which we dance, into which we return. Can we say Yes to it, can we say Yes to Christ in his death? Yes, the crucifixion is a seriously tough religious image, as tough as the Jain image of the saint as a hole, an absence, an empty outline cut out of a brass plate. Maybe even tougher: but in late medieval and Counter-Reformation times it became yet one more symbol of domination and submission to authority.

In this connection we should dwell for a moment on the non-realist reading of Jesus and his message. The sources are curious and varied, but I personally cite Kierkegaard's late *Christian Discourses* on texts from the Sermon on the Mount, Nietzsche's *Anti-Christ*, various works from the Bultmann school, and a number of excellent recent American writers, such as Sheehan, Breech, and Crossan. Here is a brief résumé of Jesus's message as a non-realist reads it.

1. *The world is passing away.* Most folk, most of the time, are well content to drift with their world and take their values from it. But what would you do if you suddenly found yourself at the end of your world, and obliged to choose absolutely?

2. *The attack upon religious objectification.* Jesus criticizes the temple, the religious professionals, tradition, and externals. Like a Cynic, he is utterly indifferent to rank and hierarchy.

3. *The hidden God.* Jesus appears to have no theology of universal human sinfulness and the need for expiation. He speaks of God in a very restrained and oblique style, using the "divine passive" construction (as in "they shall be comforted"). He privatizes or internalizes God. God is in the heart, hidden.

4. *Forgetting the past and the future.* Jesus is uninterested in the
   sort of Grand Narrative religion that draws heavily upon the
   past for legitimization and on the future for vindication. He
   wants to concentrate all attention upon the here and now.

To non-realists, it seems obvious that Christianity has during most of its history been drifting further and further away
from Jesus. There has been only one Christian so far, says
Nietzsche sourly, and he died on the cross. And Nietzsche
felt, as a number of people feel now, that there are important
and, as yet, largely unexplored possibilities in Jesus's teaching.

I return now, in conclusion, to the varieties of non-realism
in the modern period, and the difficulty that such variety may
be thought to present.

Casting one's mind back to the period around 1800 or so, a
number of different forms of non-realism can already be dis-
cerned. There is a Kantian tradition of "moral faith," which
says things like "Conscience is the voice of God," and "Faith
expresses a value-judgement," and which runs through German and Anglo-Saxon liberal Protestantism up to modern
times. There is an Hegelian, historicist version of non-realism,
for which God is an awaited future totalization of the whole
evolving world-process. There is a tradition stemming from
the younger (and less orthodox) selves of Schleiermacher and
Wordsworth that sees faith as a feeling-response of the heart
to the living Whole in which we have our being. And there is a
tradition of radical Christianity on the far left of the Reformed
tradition that crops up memorably in William Blake, and inter-
mittently in others since. It says, shortly, that God is known
only through Christ—because Jesus Christ is the only God.

These four versions of non-realism demythologize God
down into the moral demand, the goal of history, nature, and
the man Christ Jesus respectively. I could name more, being
conscious of having produced a number of distinct "positions"
myself during the past twenty-five years—four at least.

This protean quality of non-realism is exceedingly annoy-
ing to our orthodox critics, because they naturally wish to see
us clearly defined and clearly condemned in the traditional

and proper manner. They want us to stand still so that we can be shot, and they find our variety and mobility very frustrating. Why can't we keep still?

You will see by now why the difficulty arises. Orthodox realism inherits from Plato and Parmenides the belief in the ultimate unity of all truth and all values. The whole order of things is objectively coherent, both intellectually and morally, so that there is in the end One True Morality out there, which objectively coincides with the One Great Truth of all things out there. In which case every heresy ought surely to be easily definable as a minor blemish or spot on the face of the vast realist vision, and treatable accordingly.

Unfortunately, things are not as the realists would wish. Nobody has succeeded in totalizing either the history of philosophy, or the history of religions, or the history of ethics along the lines demanded by their theory. The evidence of the history of philosophy, of religions, and of moralities suggests rather that all these things are like art-products, and they cannot be finally totalized for the same reason that we cannot either finalize the definition of art or totalize its history. The very notions of orthodoxy, system, and heresy belong only to the realist vision. (Come to think of it, the very notion of "the high ground" is also realist.) So we non-realists, somehow, cannot help being mobile, errant.

3
The Practice of Post-Dogmatic Religion

5

Is Anything Sacred?: Christian Humanism and Christian Nihilism

MIRCEA ELIADE, who was born in Romania in 1907, was probably the last of the great encyclopedists of religion. He wrote a very large number of books before beginning, in 1975 at Chicago, what he expected to be his last big project, a multivolume *History of Religious Ideas*. It would cover the world from the Stone Age to the present day. He wrote a preface, with a foretaste of what he saw as the final message of his planned work. It would reveal "the profound and indivisible unity of the human mind."

Eliade had learned this theme from C. G. Jung, and it was important to him for various reasons. As a single global culture emerges, we will increasingly need a unified story of our own spiritual past; Eliade, like Jung, saw the study of archaic cultures as a way of reactivating forgotten and neglected capacities within ourselves. Our linear historical development has carried us a very long way from our origins, and has led us to think of time as being irreversible. We see it as a destroyer: it takes away, but it never gives back. In archaic cultures, though, people knew how to regenerate their lives by returning again and again into their myths and symbols. For them, time and the world were cyclical. Everything was reborn over and over, and people did not suffer as we do from the dread of time slipping away. Our age needs something of that power of renewal. So when we study the religious past of humanity we are not just looking for a unified *theory* about something that we are keeping at arm's length; we are also hoping through union with our own past for reconciliation within ourselves. Again the accent is Jungian: meeting the past, we reencounter something of the repressed depths of our own being. In the history of religions virtually everything we come across awakens an echo in our own souls, and can be profitable to us.

So far, so familiar. Eliade had been saying all this for years. Now he added something new. If we can understand the religious past better, we may perhaps get a better understanding of its strange outcome—namely, our own secular world. Eliade planned in his last chapter to discuss the modern crisis of religion and the work of Marx, Nietzsche, and Freud. This would equip us, he said, to understand "the sole, but important religious creation of the modern Western world. I refer to the ultimate stage of desacralization. The process is of considerable interest to the historian of religions, for it illustrates the complete camouflage of the 'sacred'—more precisely, its identification with the 'profane.'"[1]

Eliade was saying something like this: in virtually all earlier ages there was a clear distinction between two great realms: spirit and flesh, the sacred and the profane, the religious world and the common, secular world. In modern culture that distinction has vanished. The remaining tokens of the sacred no longer have any real power. In effect, the profane seems to have overrun the sacred, or perhaps we should say that the two domains have become one and the same. Either way, this is one of the greatest events in human history and it needs explaining. What has happened?

Eliade died before completing his project, but in the section of the book where he dealt with the rise of Christianity, he developed his argument further, pointing to something very strange in the Christian experience of revelation.[2]

For most of the ancient Jews, the Messiah, when at last he arrived, would be unmistakable. The nation would be obvi-

---

[1] Mircea Eliade, *A History of Religious Ideas*, vol. 1, *From the Stone Age to the Eleusinian Mysteries*, trans. Willard R. Trask (Chicago: University of Chicago Press, 1979), p. xvi.

[2] Eliade, *A History of Religious Ideas*, vol. 2, *From Gautama Buddha to the Triumph of Christianity*, trans. Willard R. Trask (Chicago: University of Chicago Press, 1982), pp. 359–61.

ously liberated, and the world obviously transfigured. Real revelation surely leaves no room for doubt. The epiphany of the divine, when it came, would be complete and overwhelming. But in Christianity, it did not turn out like this, and it has never been like this. Jesus was an ordinary man who suffered and died. His Messiahship and his divine Sonship were veiled, and could be rejected. His resurrection could be doubted, and his ascendedness remains unseen, a matter of faith. Ordinary secular history has continued. The church is a time-bound human institution whose history is merely a human history. If the Kingdom of God and the powers of the coming age are somehow at work in the church, then it has to be admitted that they are at work only in a hidden way. Like it or not, the whole of the Christian revelation has been veiled, ambiguous, and known only by faith. Eliade summed up: "there is here the same dialectical process that is well known in the history of religions: the epiphany of the sacred in a profane object is at the same time a camouflage; for the sacred is not *obvious* to all those who approach the object in which it has manifested itself."[3]

The principle is one that we were taught by Pascal and Kierkegaard: in revealing himself, God hides himself. In the humble and obscure man Jesus, God is more deeply hidden than he is in the glory of creation. In Christ, God is incognito. Now I am going beyond Eliade and deep into conjecture, but let us extrapolate this idea to its furthest limit: if the more God reveals himself the more he hides himself, then his completest self-revelation will coincide with his final disappearance.

That is what we have seen happen in the course of church history. Christianity was originally founded on a promise that the present darkness of faith would be only temporary. Soon the patient faithful, watching and waiting, would be rewarded. They would see the *parousia:* the visible return of Christ in glory, the triumph of God, the annihilation of evil and the end of history. But the promise was never fulfilled, and the story

---

[3] Ibid., p. 361.

of Christianity has been the story of an endless deferral. The *parousia* has been postponed and postponed *ad infinitum*. This has gradually forced the church to come to terms with history and secularity. In every generation the church's intellectual leaders find themselves having to deliver much the same message to the disappointed faithful: "Bury your faith deeper in your hearts. Settle down in time, for it's going to be a long haul. Love your neighbor: since you're not going to see Christ in person within any foreseeable future, you'd better learn to see something of him in other persons." And in effect the same message is still being delivered today, as we turn more to social ethics, banalize the liturgy, demythologize doctrine, and so on.

Thus the sacred postponed its own full arrival so often that eventually we learned that we must do without it. The promised supernatural Kingdom of God is not coming, so we had better try to build some sort of substitute for it ourselves, in this age and out of secular materials.

This interpretation of the meaning of secularization owes much to Albert Schweitzer, and it tries to show why it all happened within the very heart of Christian culture. Eliade could perhaps in his last chapter have taken the argument one stage further, following T. J. J. Altizer (e.g., *History as Apocalypse*, S.U.N.Y., 1985) and Thomas Sheehan (*The First Coming*, Vintage, 1988). These writers radicalize the message of the incarnation of God in Christ. This event bridged the gap between heaven and earth. It implied that henceforth the divine was human and the human was divine. God has become what we are in order that we may become what he is. In Christ the divine has completely and finally disappeared into the human, so that there no longer is and no longer needs to be any separate sacred realm. The moral development of Christianity was strangely slow and it took a very long time to accept fully the holiness of the human body, but, as Altizer points out, in French Gothic cathedral sculpture this was belatedly achieved. At Chartres and Reims, the body is both completely human and fully holy, and Christianity reaches its goal as the

religion that ends religion, and the faith in which the spiritual
history of humanity is rounded off.

Another visual illustration: in the sixteenth century, Christian humanism developed a stage further. The Protestant Reformation from 1517 and the Catholic Reformation from the
Council of Trent (1545–1563) began the long process of raising the value of ordinary lay life in the world, and in particular
the value of Christian marriage, motherhood, and family life.
It was against this background that Titian, during the early
1570s and in his own extreme old age, made the painting of a
mother and child that now belongs to the National Gallery in
London. The painting is undocumented, and nobody knows
for sure whether it was originally intended as a religious painting of the Virgin and Child, and, of course, the point is that the
question is unimportant. In the painting, the old, venerated
symbol of Mary the Virgin and her child Jesus becomes universal human motherhood, both common and holy. Looking
at the painting, one understands that the destiny of the labeled sacred object is to come to a point at which, in order to
finish its job of transfiguring human experience, it must lose
its separate identity and its name. It must be dispersed into
humanity at large. So Christianity is always in the process of
secularizing itself, passing into the human, losing its identity
and becoming common property. That is redemption.

We are now ready to take up the question posed in my title:
is anything sacred? I've been suggesting that the secularism
of the modern world is indeed a religious phenomenon, that
it is a product of Christianity, and that it points to a *dialectical*
interpretation of Christianity. Yes, Christianity does indeed
start out by positing certain sacred objects and themes—but
only in order to secularize them and so make them belong to
everyone.

The story, to recapitulate, goes as follows: In Christianity
the promised unambiguous self-manifestation and self-vindi-
cation of the sacred never happened. Instead, God remained
off-stage and secular history went on. The only revelation
Christianity has ever had is a revelation of God hidden in
human form, hidden under bread and wine, and so forth. What

is distinctive about the Christian God is the way he veils himself, gives himself, dies, and passes away into universal human experience.

Christianity is dialectical in that it is always in movement between two poles. It starts by saying that this, this, and this are holy—but only in order to end by saying that everything human is holy. It is as if God exists not for his own sake, but only for ours. There is already a hint of this humanist reversal of traditional religious thought in Jesus's saying, "The sabbath was made for man, not man for the sabbath; so the son of man [presumably, the ordinary human being] is lord even of the sabbath" (Mark 2:27).

Is anything sacred? Yes: there is a universal sacredness in our life. At least, there is if we are talking about the Christian humanism that flourished from the thirteenth to the nineteenth centuries. Christian humanists continue to affirm the great christological doctrines, keep the feasts, and use the symbols because all these things are meant to become universal and true of every human being.

When at Christmas my skeptical colleagues crowd into carol services and nativity plays with their children, I do not suppose for a moment that they actually believe the popular supernaturalism of the stories. No: they see the story of Christ's nativity as a symbolism under which we can renew our sense of the holiness of the common human experience of childbirth and family life.

The Christian humanism that we have been describing so far has gone through many phases—Gothic, Renaissance, Baroque, Romantic. My interpretation of it comes principally from Hegel. I do not want to attack it. So far as it can still be made to work, I am all in favor of it. But I fear that it is now on the way out. The Enlightenment brought new understandings of the human person, of religion, and of history that, by the end of the nineteenth century, had led to an acute crisis. Critical historical thinking had realized the transient, historically-produced character of every human system of thought. All was fictional. But was that realization itself a fiction? An abyss opened.

The new event was that people, just a few of them, glimpsed nihilism. They saw that we are in the void and we make the lot. Language and culture come first, and they form everything. Apart from our language, our values, our cultural forms, and our interpretations, there is only formless and meaningless white noise. But our language, our forms, and our interpretations are purely contingent products of history. In no way are they guaranteed or privileged. True, our ways of thinking, our scientific theories, and so on, seem to us today to work; but other ideas seemed to work yesterday, and tomorrow people will doubtless think differently again. All our theories, beliefs, and values are merely projections upon the void: they are just our transient fictions, invented by us to give our life value.

This glimpse of nihilism was, I believe, a great event. It spread very rapidly in the world of ideas. In religion it marked a break. The older Christian humanism lost its force when we recognized that it was not a genuine demythologizing of Christianity, but itself just another human myth. We were trying through it to dignify ourselves, to pull ourselves up by our own bootstraps. Now we see that the encounter with the Void has to be our way of participating in the death of Christ, and the subsequent realization of life's utter gratuitousness is our way of experiencing Grace and participating in the resurrection of Christ. For us non-realist Christians, passing through the Nihil has been a religious experience of death and rebirth. The old Christian humanism has been undercut, and something much more austere has taken its place.

We are in a strange, novel region now, and we are only just beginning to develop a new religious vocabulary. So again I raise the question: is there anything sacred? After nihilism, when everything is contingent and fleeting, what is there for Christian art to represent and for the Christian vocabulary to be *about?* Is there still an art that is both truthful and genuinely religious? I believe there is, and I shall describe its typical mood and style as the Abstract Sacred. The Abstract Sacred is not quite the personal God of the older Western tradition, nor is it quite the Void of Buddhism. It is somewhere between the two. But it is not a substance, not a thing. It cannot be represented directly. It hasn't even got an iconography of its own. To people who are familiar with the older tradition of religious artifacts that had to follow strictly defined iconographical rules in order to be readable, the Abstract Sacred must seem very paradoxical. I need to explain what this new religious art is and how it arose.

The clue to understanding what has happened to religious art in modern times is the curious and easily overlooked fact that our present notion of art dates back only as far as the middle of the eighteenth century. As part of the general Enlightenment modernization of the culture, the various fine arts, *les beaux arts* (painting, sculpture, poetry, dance, music, architecture) were for the first time all grouped together. This brought into being Art with a capital A, newly enthroned as the highest-ranking cultural pursuit. Art was defined in terms of its relation to the creativity of the human beings who produced it and the sensibility of the other human beings who enjoyed it. The new word *aesthetics* was coined, by the philosopher Baumgarten, for theory of art—meaning, roughly, the science of the way art works affect our sensibility.

Art thus came to be understood in secular humanist terms. There developed a cult of human creativity, and of pride in one's own country's artistic traditions. Art was classified into national schools. It became something to be exhibited free of charge in public national galleries, which were like shrines dedicated to the human spirit. Art was taught in academies, its history began to be constructed, and it was theorized about by critics and philosophers. Art was good for you. It was also expensive, and if you were a rich and important person, it was your duty to have a cultivated taste in it.

To be fitted into this new cultural set-up, the older Christian works of art had to be completely reinterpreted. They came to be seen not as functional church objects, but as expressions of the human religious impulse. At the same time, religion, too, was rethought in terms of the human subject. People began to talk for the first time about "religious experience," "religious feeling," and "mysticism." Religion was becoming a human function, a mode of human sensibility.

The upshot is that religious art for us moderns is no longer quite the old ecclesiastical art, defined in terms of the patron who commissioned it, the iconography it obeyed, and the religious function it served. Religious art has broken loose and become unsectarian. It can be any sort of art that arouses religious feelings in the contemplative spectator. The spectator is no longer quite using the art object according to canonical rules and *as religion*, but rather is receptive to its effect upon the feelings *as religious art*. Because of this shift, an altarpiece that once stood in a church and focused the prayers of the faithful may now in good conscience be aesthetically enjoyed in a gallery. You can have entirely creditable religious feelings in response to it, even though it has been drastically torn out of the old sacred realm for which it was originally made. In just the same way, people nowadays listen to a setting of the Mass performed in a concert hall and visit churches as architectural monuments. Furthermore, because religion and religious art are now defined in terms of our own feeling-response to them, and are therefore seen in much less immediate and dogmatically exclusive terms than formerly, our taste can range widely. We can and do get religious pleasure from a vast range of materials, from other faiths and periods, that might once have been denounced as heathen idols. We are no longer iconoclastic; that is, we no longer react with religious revulsion and horror to other people's religious images. Instead we enjoy them—as religious art.

However, we pay a price for this catholicity of taste and enjoyment. In order to enjoy the religious artifacts of the past, we have had to learn to read them historically as datable products of evolving human stylistic traditions. For example, when we view the window tracery or the rib vaulting in a medieval church, we date it and place it in a historical sequence. But this very maneuver by which we interpret the old Christian tradition and make it accessible to ourselves also prevents us from continuing it. For the old iconography no longer conducts us directly to sacred Beings in the heavenly world; it merely stands at a certain point in a historical series. This in turn means that modern religious art has to be very different in type from the Christian art of earlier times.

Vincent van Gogh, in the asylum at Saint Rémy in the autumn of 1889, was thinking much about religious subjects— for example, Christ in Gethsemane. But, as everyone knows, he ended up leaving Christ out and painting only the writhing olive trees, because a painting of Christ wouldn't quite succeed in being a portrayal of Christ himself. It would merely be a parody or a variation upon a familiar theme from the history of art. We would not be led by van Gogh's work to think directly about Christ; we would merely find ourselves thinking about the long line of earlier representations of the *Agony in the Garden* in the history of Christian art. The awareness that it, too, was only a product of history seems to have robbed the old standard Christian iconography of its former authority. So van Gogh left the human figures out of the painting; he wrote (December 1889) to Emile Bernard, "One can try to give an impression of anguish without aiming straight at the historic garden of Gethsemane." He similarly left Christ out of the *Raising of Lazarus* (May 1890). And all this was consistent with a long-declared policy. The celebrated *Potato Eaters* of April 1885 reworked the Supper at Emmaus as a simple peasant meal, and the *Still Life with Open Bible* of October 1885 showed Zola's grim secular novel *Joie de Vivre* as the true modern counterpart of the fifty-third chapter of the Book of the Prophet Isaiah. Messianic suffering is now dispersed into general human suffering.

Van Gogh was saying then that, paradoxically, if a modern work of art is to be authentically religious today, it cannot be religious in the old sense. It must look secular. The agony of the olive trees, the peasant meal, and the afflicted woman of the drawing *Sorrow* must be enough for us. And that is part of what I mean by the Abstract Sacred. After the Enlightenment, we found that the very moves by which we had made the old religious iconographies intelligible to ourselves also made it impossible for us to continue them *as religion*. We had irreversibly become like those eighteenth-century ladies and gentlemen who clucked over ruined abbeys, grottoes, and hermits. We are all of us now Heritage-Christians, tourists of religion, looking respectfully at the lovingly preserved relics of a lost past. We quickly fall into the mood of those people who, after much searching, decide that the only unembarrassing Christmas card they can find to send is a reproduction of a medieval manuscript illumination. Among such people, culture-conservatives, nostalgia for faith is only too easily mistaken for faith itself.

Our present argument, however, suggests that an authentic modern religious art must not be in any way revivalist. It must break with historicism and nostalgia for tradition. That is surely why a good deal of high Modernist and Abstract Expressionist art does strike people today as being authentically religious. Purged of subjectivity and romantic nostalgia, and without any reference to established iconographies, it is able to acquire a special kind of impersonal and objective weight and presence. As is well known, Mondrian and Kandinsky both hoped that through abstraction it might be possible for art once more to communicate spiritual values. How successful they themselves were is perhaps disputable; but for me and surely for many other people, the great works of Jackson Pollock, Barnett Newman, Ad Rhinehart, Mark Rothko, Yves Klein, and others are highly religious. They are expressions of what I am calling the Abstract Sacred.

This, however, is a new kind of sacred, for these works are not like the old Eastern Christian icons. They are post-platonic. They are not windows upon eternity. You do not use them as openings into the supernatural world. They do not point to anything else. They are not even works of religious humanism. They are flat, really flat. This sacred is abstract in two senses: there is no imagery, and there is no other-world-beyond. Instead you stop on this surface, a little perhaps like a Buddhist meditating on a flower. Substance dissolves away, and the ego dissolves away. There is only this, the Abstract Sacred, flux, void, this-ness, secularity, dispersal.

Notoriously, such art has proved extremely stressful and costly for the artist to produce. But modern religion just *is* costly, as is perhaps indicated in a different way by the work of Käthe Kollwitz. Kollwitz was active in Berlin during the first forty-odd years of this century. She was a strong humanist, who portrayed anonymous human suffering with a very fiercely controlled grief. Somehow she would not allow suffering to be in any way whatever justified, idealized, transfigured, or altered. The result is, to me, something extraordinary: *the total absence of any religious consolation is itself what makes the work religious!* That is the paradox of twentieth-century religious naturalism. The Abstract Sacred demands truth to things as they are, and a rigorous refusal to accept the lie of otherworldliness. We must be saints of the earth.

The paradoxes are multiplying. Van Gogh found that if it is to be effectively Christian nowadays, art must leave out Christ himself. To be truly religious, it must be "flat," entirely of this world and quite unconsoled. The Abstract Sacred gets its religious weight from its very repudiation of the supernatural, a point eloquently made in the work of Richard Long. When people compare Long's works of landscape art with megalithic monuments, the comparison only draws attention to the uncompromising horizontality of Long's work. From Babylonian ziggurats and Stonehenge to Victorian spires, through almost five millennia, religion had pointed upward toward a higher world. Long's chosen materials, rocks and mud, stood at the bottom of the old Chain of Being. They could not be more than a launch-pad for the soul. Long, however, really does want us to stop at them. They are not to be used as mere jumping-off points: in Long's work the Abstract Sacred stays on the land surface, and we should stay there, too.

Long makes almost no provision for the conservation of his work. He produces little in the way of saleable commodity-art. His works are made as he passes by and then left to fade, so that they can be read as symbols of human transience. How are they able to give us such a strong sense of the sacred? By, I think, their austerity and impersonality, and by their matter-of-fact acceptance of their own transience. They seem to speak to us of an enduring, unnamable Background against which our brief life is acted out. But this Background, this Abstract Sacred, must not be reified, nor must it be thought of as an Eternal One. It is something for which we have no developed vocabulary, but of which art has made us aware. It may be a starting point for the religion of the future.

6

The Human Condition: Diagnosis and Therapy

WHEN WE BEGIN to study a new religious tradition, such as Hinduism, we soon discover that we must learn a few foreign words that have no English counterparts. Each great tradition of faith is a distinctive way of thinking. To get into it, you have to familiarize yourself with a number of basic concepts. What makes these terms basic is the fact that the way they work gives the key to the way the entire system works. Once you have got hold of them, you can find your way around.

Learning a new cluster of basic ideas is hard work. They seem very opaque at first. But it is also curiously difficult to recognize the basic concepts of one's own tradition, and even harder to absorb the idea that they are breaking down. Things so deeply familiar that we are unaware of them have suddenly become exotic and strange, from within as it were. That's hard to take. In the past decade or so we have seen many new words and phrases introduced, phrases such as "the end of history," "anti-realism" and "post-modernism." These terms draw attention to something very odd that is happening within our own culture. But they are not in the dictionary, and they have not been stabilized by many years of public use. At this stage, everyone who uses words like "realism" and "non-realism" seems to be using them slightly differently. The terms of the debate are still contested, and there isn't any canonical pattern of use to appeal to.

Many people become most indignant about all the neologisms currently flying around. They think the whole debate must surely be a waste of time. According to them, if something is worth saying then it can be said clearly—which means that they want it to be said in familiar words. They feel insulted and perhaps excluded when they hear new words being used. They don't like the challenge to their own deep assumptions. The anger that new words can arouse resembles the anger caused by innovations in art.

I rather sympathize with this annoyance. I hate having to cudgel my brains to make sense of bad and obscure writing, and I try to avoid ever recommending such books to students. But the position for about a century now has been that our whole tradition of philosophy, religion, and morality is being sharply questioned. Profound changes are afoot. This inevitably means that people are proposing new basic concepts, trying out new vocabulary. We just cannot avoid a certain amount of linguistic difficulty and confusion. At least for the present.

So we must keep talking around the issues and trying out new angles. Gradually we'll become clearer, and a new vocabulary will become settled.

How then are we to characterize the change that is taking place? Many people have a rough idea of the answer: all the deep assumptions that were entrenched in our culture by Plato are now being challenged. But they are not being replaced by a new set of assumptions of the same general sort. Rather, we are changing over from what I shall call "dogma" to what I'll call "therapy." We're not just changing over from dogmatic to critical thinking, from unexamined assumptions to examined ones. Rather, our outlook is becoming entirely beliefless and foundationless.

To explain this, let's begin with the traditional complaint that our life is too short, uncertain, and unhappy. Nothing lasts as long as we would like it to. Reality, truth, goodness, and happiness are never unmixed. The passage of time gradually takes everything away from us. Our dissatisfaction with life can be the cause of great distress to us. What are we to do about it? We look to philosophy and religion for help. The help can take one of two forms. The teacher may take our complaint at face value and meet it by telling us the good news that there is a better world for us elsewhere. This better world is a world of supreme and unchanging Reality, perfection and happiness. It is the True World, so that the teaching about it is a proportionately higher kind of truth than truth about the world of sense. The teacher tells us how we can get to this better world, and there enjoy a blessed immortality. So this teacher simply accepts our complaints. Yes, he says, you are quite right to complain as you do about transience, suffering, and death. Your very complaint shows that this present world of ours is not your true home and not the place where you should be. You were made for something better. You are currently exiled from your true home and stuck in a world of shadowy appearances, but I'm going to tell you how to get to the Real World where you belong.

That's what I call "dogma."

But there is an alternative approach. Again we voice all the same complaints about transience, suffering, and death. We moan about living in a half-world in which reality, truth, goodness, and happiness are never as fully delivered to us as we would wish. And so on. However, this time the teacher reacts differently: instead of telling us that our complaints are justified and we can trade in this world for a better one, he replies to us in the manner of a physician or counselor. Why are we so unhappy? What is causing us to complain, and is it possible to cure our complaints by removing the factors that caused us to make them?

This style of teaching is what I call therapy. The teacher doesn't set out to meet the complaint directly; instead he treats it as symptomatic. He tries to diagnose it and treat its causes. The dogmatic teacher gives an answer, but the therapist aims for a cure. Both teachers are concerned about salvation, but they mean different things by it. The dogmatic teacher conveys saving truths about how to get out of this unsatisfactory world and into a better world. Salvation is then redemption from this world. It's a *transfer*. Whereas for the therapist, salvation consists in being restored to yourself, to good health in this world and this life. Salvation is like being cured of an illness or a neurosis. You are not given any extra knowledge or higher truth; you are simply returned to yourself, and reunited with your own life. Whereas the dogmatic teacher believes in two worlds, one apparent and the other Real, the therapist believes in only one world.

In the western tradition so far, much of our philosophy and most of our religious thinking have been of the dogmatic type. Ever since Plato, we have been heavily influenced by the appearance-reality distinction. The job of religion and philosophy has been to make up for the unsatisfactoriness of this fleeting world by supplying us with additional, unchanging, and specially-important higher Truths to steer by and hold on to. There was an invisible order beyond the world of sense. Philosophy portrayed it as a world of necessary truth and eternal values and meanings. Religion portrayed it simply as Heaven, the supernatural world. Either way, the invisible order supported everything, gave everything value, and made everything intelligible.

It is because of this background that so many people still think that our salvation depends upon having a creed or a philosophy—which in turn means holding a set of extra-important convictions about an invisible, superior order of things. This life and this world are indeed unsatisfactory, but in the world above you can find the eternal perfection and truth and happiness that your soul longs for, and indeed was created for. Furthermore, most of us in the West have supposed that a faith of this type is needed in order to make life worth living. Life here below is wretched, and only dogma can help: that's what we've thought.

However, during the nineteenth century, two-worlds dualism, and therefore also the dogmatic style of teaching, began to break down. The story of how and why this happened is very familiar, but I'll just mention a few of the key arguments.

The first argument is that every natural language is purely human, historically-evolving, and bound into a human way of life. Language is a continuum in which every part is related to every other. There is no way in which one and the same natural language could function in two different worlds, one temporal and the other eternal, one bodily and the other spiritual, and so forth. There is simply no sense in the claim that our language could address itself to any other world than this one.

Secondly—and it's a related argument—"the best criticism of dogma is the history of dogma." That is to say, although people may claim that their beliefs, philosophical, religious, and ethical, are unchanging absolutes, it is now clear that all such beliefs are just human and changing, and have human histories. Historical study shows every supposed absolute to be just relative.

Thirdly, the old two-worlds doctrine implied that human beings came in two parts. A bit of us belongs to the natural world here below, but we have special capacities—rational, moral, and spiritual—that put us in touch with a higher world beyond space and time. Thus a human being was seen as a mix of nature and spirit, body and soul. However, in recent years I believe we have found good reason to reject such dualism. Instead we have come to adopt a much more unified picture of the human being as one formed all the way through by culture and language.

Nowadays we believe in one world only, a historically-developing continuum of language-formed experience, in which we live immersed. The result is that we are moving over to the therapeutic model of what religious teaching is and how it works. Religion and philosophy don't tell us about a better world beyond, and they don't give us extra information of a superior sort. Instead they work to cure our discontent and reconcile us to this world. They don't save us from the world or from ourselves; they save us by giving us back to ourselves. You are saved when you feel that you are completely at one with your own life, and able to say Yes to it.

Of the great thinkers and teachers of the past, the one who best typifies the therapeutic approach is probably the Buddha. The commentators tell us that the basic summary of his central teachings, the Four Holy Truths, is cast in medical form. First, you must present your diagnosis of what is wrong with the patient; secondly, you must define the causes of the illness; thirdly, you must say whether the disease is curable; and finally, you must spell out the way to achieve the cure. Following this pattern, the Buddha teaches that all human life is pervaded by suffering of various kinds. The cause of this suffering is clinging, craving, or attachment. The cure for suffering lies in the removal of its causes, and the way to achieve this is by following the eight-fold path.

The Buddha often emphasizes that his approach is purely therapeutic. "Both in the past and now, I teach just this: suffering and the cessation of suffering." He is content to leave open the great metaphysical questions that trouble Westerners, such as whether there is a Creator or not. His purpose is purely soteriological; that is, he teaches a way to salvation. He doesn't teach dogmatically, and the state of salvation, *nibbana* or *nirvana*, is described chiefly in negative terms. We know that it is the cessation of suffering, but otherwise the nature of nibbana is left largely undetermined.

All this helps to explain a paradox in Western attitudes to Buddhism. Westerners tend to equate religion with dogmatic belief, especially belief in God, spirits, Grace, and life after death. Learning that Buddhism is unconcerned with such matters, Westerners are liable to respond by saying that in that case, Buddhism can't really be a religion at all: it should perhaps rather be described as a philosophy, or a way of life. But this is an oddly misguided thing to say. The position is that Buddhism is an exceptionally pure religion, which concentrates entirely on the quest for salvation. It is therapeutic, practical—and *therefore* strikingly dogma-less. Buddhism suggests that the purest religion will be the one with the least beliefs. If your religion has really saved you, so that you are able to accept yourself and your life, then you'll feel no need for beliefs.

Even before the birth of Christ, Hellenistic kings debated with Buddhist philosophers. But it has taken a very long time for us to absorb the Buddhist message. During the nineteenth century, Western thinking was steadily becoming more post-metaphysical, this-worldly, humanist, and then pragmatist. But the leading nineteenth-century thinkers have still not grasped the idea of therapy as an alternative to dogma, and

Schopenhauer, Nietzsche, and William James all see Buddhism as pessimistic. Only with the later Wittgenstein does Western thought at last achieve a really clear statement of the therapeutic outlook, and therefore draw close to Buddhism.

Since the 1960s, Wittgenstein's philosophy has encouraged Western thinkers to attempt a fresh interpretation of the Madhyamika, the "Middle Way." Wittgenstein, to put it rather crudely, held that if you take a non-realistic view of language and the part it plays in our lives, you can avoid a great many disabling and uncomfortable philosophical illusions. Therapeutic philosophy is a practice that seeks to cure people of philosophical errors. In a similar vein, Mahayana Buddhist teaching says that a mistaken view of language leads people to believe in an objective world, out there beyond language, whose structure, they believe, must reflect the structure of language. Most people thus fall into an excessively objectifying way of thinking, and even a kind of fetishism. In this version of Buddhism, the *tanha*, or craving that causes all our suffering, is realism itself, a fixated attachment to illusory thought-objects that have been generated by a mistaken philosophy of language. Buddhist religious practice has therefore the same purpose as Wittgenstein's philosophical practice. It is therapy for realism. Salvation is freedom from bondage to fixated or fetishistic desire.

Notice that on this account Buddhist therapy is not setting out to cure us of the passions as such, but only of the fixation of the passions that occurs when we take too realistic a view of the world. We get a good indication of the change that is occurring in our interpretation of Buddhism if we consider the different words that have been used to translate *tanha*. The Buddha seeks "the cessation of *tanha*"—but what is it? A century ago, the translator might have written "desire," but since the complete cessation of desire occurs only in death, this translation suggests a highly pessimistic interpretation of the Buddha's gospel. Fifty years ago, the translator might have written "craving," suggesting that we should seek freedom only from futile and inordinate desire. Today, the translator is very likely to write "clinging," meaning that we should learn to stop clutching at illusory pseudo-objects.

Thus the older severely-ascetic interpretation of Buddhism is tending to give way to an anti-realistic interpretation of Buddhism. We can gain freedom and happiness by escaping from false absolutes, and from all objectifying and fixated ways of thinking.

Having got this far, we can now detect rather similar themes in the Christian tradition. The polemic against idolatry was also aiming to free people from their bad habit of clutching at illusory pseudo-objects. The old doctrine, that this world is coming to an end and the believer should flee from it, can be read in an anti-realist sense. It warns people not to become hooked upon things that are passing away. We are not talking about leaving the world altogether, a meaningless idea, but about being delivered from bondage to the world. Too realistic a view of the world-order and worldly objects is a kind of idolatry that holds people captive and makes them wretched. They need liberation.

However, there is another and even more important parallel between Buddhism and Christianity that the therapeutic approach highlights. Recent thought has stressed that all languages and cultures structure experience by setting up binary contrasts. Typical ones are male and female, sun and moon, land and sea, plant and animal, yes and no, right-hand and left-hand, affirmation and negation, the wild and the tame, clean and unclean, heaven and earth, the saved and the lost, up and down, conservative and reformist, flesh and spirit, reason and the passions, church and state, time and eternity, and so on. It seems that we have no option but to operate in terms of this binary logic of yes and no, this and that, the preferred and the rejected, the dominant and the subordinate.

But the consequence is that, in all sorts of ways, our loyalties become divided and our experience fragmented. Accordingly, one principal aim of philosophical and religious teachings is to re-integrate the self by "mediating" or reconciling all the various oppositions. And this is a particularly prominent theme in all doctrines of salvation. To gain happiness, we must integrate our concerns and allegiances. To do this we must follow a therapeutic way of life that will gradually achieve a union of the opposites.

So here we have a fresh angle on the contrast between dogma and therapy. Dogma is cosmological. It sets out to structure the real in terms of binary oppositions. It distinguishes, for example, between this world and the next world, profane love and sacred love, honoring one's parents and honoring God, secular and religious obligation, the short-term and the long-term. But every time we set up a distinction of this sort, we create a conflict of loyalties. Cosmological divisions produce moral division within our lives. So the therapeutic principle tries to heal the divisions and join everything up again. Eternal life can be lived in the here and now, it says. The love of God and the love of one's fellow human can become one and the same—and so on.

Look at the paradox: dogma divides, to produce a scaled real order of things as the object of belief. Therapy heals the divisions, undoing the effects of belief. Salvation lies in a certain wholeness or integration of selfhood, way of life, and world-view. To achieve it, we must unite the opposites.

In Mahayana Buddhism, the classic statement of this principle is by Nagarjuna. *Samsara* means the cycles of birth and death, and *nirvana* is the goal of the spiritual life. They roughly correspond to what the West calls things temporal and things eternal, and Nagarjuna brings them sharply together:

> Samsara is nothing essentially different from nirvana. Nirvana is nothing essentially different from samsara.
> The limits of nirvana are the limits of samsara. Between the two, also, there is not the slightest difference whatsoever.

In and through meditation, Nagarjuna is saying, we should reach a moment in which we are able to say that this purely contingent fleeting here-and-now is the supreme goal of the religious life. I have only to add one cautionary note: salvation is more than just saying, "This is it." Salvation is to have followed the path until you have earned the right to say: "This is it."

In the later Mahayana tradition, this idea of religion as a therapy that leads us to salvation by uniting the opposites is taken a good deal further. The Japanese master Dogen, a contemporary of Thomas Aquinas, is the best example. His entire teaching has been summarized in eleven identities that we should seek to realize. They are the identity of self and others, of practice with Enlightenment, of life and death, of time and being, of men and women, and so on. Salvation is a blissful, non-dualistic mode of being and vision of the world. Dogen's words immediately remind us of many very close Western parallels, as when he says: "One speck of dust is nirvana."

How then might we describe a therapeutic interpretation of Christianity? It is there in the tradition, and quite easy to spell out. We should give up the grand cosmological claims and the realistic dogma. Instead we should concentrate on salvation, summarizing the way to it in a series of identity-statements like Dogen's:

> Identity of loving God and loving one's neighbor.
> Identity of faith and works.
> Identity of this life and Eternal life.
> Identity of the holy and the common.
> Identity of perfect self-affirmation and perfect self-surrender.
> Identity of time and eternity.
> Identity of dying and living.
> Identity of creativity and receptivity.

And so on. Thus we may learn to see religion, not as giving us supplementary information about another realm of being, but as a practice that strives to reconcile and integrate our way of life and our world-view. It is a beliefless religion, and therefore the true religion.

7

Spirituality, Old and New

DURING THE PAST DECADE or so, as instant communication between people in different parts of the world has become
cheaper and cheaper, it has often occurred to me that we need
to begin developing a global religious vocabulary. Because the
Universal Declaration of Human Rights of 1948 was signed up to
at the time by most countries, it has done a very good job in
helping us to develop at least the beginnings of a global *moral*
vocabulary. Talk about human rights may sound rather different in different countries of the world, and may be very unpopular in some places, but it has by now acquired a certain
universal resonance and moral authority. No country, however
arrogant and isolationist, likes to have a bad reputation in the
field of human rights. And with the United Nations Organiza-
tion there have also become established a number of international bodies such as the ILO and the WHO, whose work has
done much to establish a common moral vocabulary, values,
and goals across the world. The way we have come to use the
word "humanitarian" is a good illustration of what has been
achieved. Countries with very different cultural traditions
have begun to talk a moral language which is not just local,
but global. And this development is not a mere luxury, but a
necessity if we are to negotiate worldwide about such matters
as international law, the environment, and population policy.

Some progress has then been made in establishing a global
and humanistic moral vocabulary, and if this has been a good
and necessary thing then shouldn't we also be looking for the
development of a global *religious* vocabulary? Humanity's ancient faiths are all tied to particular geographical regions, languages, and histories to such an extent that religious
allegiance frequently looks like the nationalism with which it
is so often bound up. It is not universal, but highly specific,

jealous, and exclusive. It very often leads communities to draw apart from each other, to eye each other suspiciously, and even to come into conflict. But in the modern age, most larger states have become multi-faith, and all faiths alike are now threatened by rapid cultural change. Isn't it becoming urgent that the major world faiths should begin to talk to each other, and to develop a common vocabulary in which they can find common ground and make common cause? Various faiths claim to be "catholic" or universal, but in practice none yet is so. A generally-accepted world religious vocabulary will surely help all the faiths to escape from their respective cultural ghettos, expand their sympathies, become *porous* and mingle with and into each other. Surely the old obsession with maintaining separate vocabularies and separate identities, unpolluted by each other, is now out of date?

So far, so good. What will be the key words in a world religious vocabulary?

This is not an easy question to answer. Everybody knows that in all faith communities since the Second World War there has been a strong tendency to put up the shutters, resist assimilation, and retreat into various forms of neo-orthodoxy or traditionalism. People simply do not *want* to change their ways. In Christianity, the ecumenical movement has ground to a halt; and on the wider front, bodies such as the World Congress of Faiths have few achievements to point to. Everywhere, religious vocabularies and doctrines are more likely to be used as badges of difference and separation, rather than to negotiate agreements. About the most that can be said is this—that, as in ethics, our struggle to establish a global moral vocabulary will probably begin with such words as *humanism*, *humanitarianism* and *human rights*, so in religion, about all that we have to start with is words like *spirit, spiritual values* and *spirituality*. While in order to link ethics and religion, we have also agreed that among human rights there are certain religious rights, which are now widely claimed and conceded: the right to assemble, to worship, and generally to practice and to propagate one's religion freely.

What then *do* the religions have in common today? So far as public discourse is concerned, it seems that the answer is that they have a common interest in battling against *anti*-religion and against something usually called "materialism." Hence, perhaps, the popularity of talk about "the spirit," about "body, mind, and spirit," about "spiritual values," and about "spirituality." When we use this language we are drawing upon the old contrast between spirit and matter. We are trying to gather a broad multi-faith constituency in support of the proposition that "materialism," whatever that is, is a very Bad Thing, and that in religion we concern ourselves with another and larger realm that transcends the material world. The presumption is that we are all of us today threatened by thorough-going secularism, and that a purely this-worldly outlook and way of life is a state of bondage. Talk about the spirit and spirituality is talk about how human beings can be liberated from captivity to "the world" and material things.

In all this, the presumption is that the essential message of religion, and the one thing that must at all costs be preserved, is the picture of the human being as an amphibian. Our life is a journey through time toward our true and final home in the eternal world. We are composed of two parts, the body, or "the flesh," and the soul, or spirit. In human life and human society there are two realms that presently coexist: Nature and Grace, the secular and the sacred, Throne and Altar, the civil and the ecclesiastical, things human and things divine, the relative and the absolute, time and eternity, outward appearance and invisible inner reality. Everywhere, religion is assumed to be concerned with a distinct and higher-ranking sphere of life and dimension of human existence. The assumption is that today, "materialism" threatens this ancient world-view and thereby threatens human dignity and the very survival of the human spirit. And if this is right, it would seem that when we talk about spiritual values and spirituality, we are saying that the essence of all religion is Platonism, the concern for an eternal Reality beyond the passing show of material existence, an eternal Reality in which we shall at last find our true home.

Against this background, I can now state the dilemma that I propose to discuss in this lecture. It is often complained that

much modern talk about spirituality is wishy-washy and self-
serving. What does it all amount to? Is it just fantasy? In reply,
I am suggesting that words like *spirit*, *spiritual*, and *spirituality*
still get their meaning chiefly from various ancient oppositions
that are deeply embedded in our culture: the biblical contrast
between the flesh, which is weak, and the power of the spirit;
the old medieval contrast between "the spirituality" (that is,
the clergy) and such "temporalities" as property and money;
the pervasive contrast between a person's outward appearance
and her hidden, "interior," and "spiritual" life—and so on.
Out of this background has gradually developed our own use
of the word "spirituality" to mean "concern for a Higher, religious, dimension of human existence." We often also speak of
"*a* spirituality," in the sense of a specific religious *style*, a particular set of religious practices and attitudes that some individual or group has evolved and lives by.

Thus, if people complain that talk about spirituality is horri-
bly vague, I answer that we can learn at least something of its
meaning from its history. In practice, this means learning what
spirit means by looking at what it has been contrasted with.
Spirit is power, as opposed to the weakness of the flesh. The
world of the spirit is unchanging and eternal, as opposed to
this world of time and change. Spirit is inward and hidden
reality, as opposed to the outward appearance of the body and
clothing. And so on. But now we see that everything we say
about the history of things spiritual is highly dualistic, whereas
today, when people are talking about spirituality, they almost
invariably disclaim any intention to confirm the old opposition
between this world and the next world, between outer and
inner, body and soul, secular and Sacred, time and eternity,
and the rest.

The dilemma, then, is this: it is very difficult to use any
religious vocabulary today without invoking a history of extreme two-worlds dualism that one must hasten to disclaim.
Most religious liberals today try to go on using the traditional
religious vocabulary, while at the same time repudiating the
old cosmological beliefs and valuations that used to give that

vocabulary meaning. It is no wonder that we end up sounding vague, woolly, and confused.

Most of our religious vocabulary first came into use around 20–25 centuries ago, at a time of very deep pessimism about the possibility of human life in this world ever being entirely happy. The only way to make life bearable was to suppose that we must be cosmic prisoners-of-war, held captive under miserable conditions by a foreign power, namely, Satan—or even, as some have thought, in an entirely foreign world. As it is, nothing is right: here in our captivity, time drags heavily along, but our true home is not in time at all. We belong in the eternal world above. These corruptible mortal bodies of ours are only a kind of prison clothing that we are temporarily forced to wear. Our true identities are now hidden inside us, and will only become fully manifest when we get Home. All the ambient conditions of our life are at present wretched, and the whole cultural world of symbolic communication within which we now live is Vanity Fair: outward show, illusion, deception, and folly. But we *will* be delivered.

Thus the whole of the present set-up within which human beings are living is relegated to the status of a mere outward and perishing appearance. On the day of salvation what is now hidden and inward will stand forth and be publicly manifested as having all along been the true and eternal reality of things. Meanwhile there are on earth a few colonies in which elect people live a special way of life that is an anticipation or foreshadowing of the Real life that is to come; and these colonies are the religious orders of men and of women.

Now a spirituality was, in the past at least, a set of practices through which you regularly acted out and reconfirmed your vision of the world and the human condition. Christian spirituality, from about the third century to the nineteenth, passed a comprehensively hostile judgement upon almost every aspect of human life in this world. It then invoked the philosophers' contrast between appearance and reality, declaring that this present evil world is only appearance and doomed soon to perish. The Real World and the blessed way of life yet to come is already being acted out and anticipated in the lives of monks and nuns. They are the top grade of holy persons, in most religions. But lay people living in this present world can also practice a spirituality by being inwardly monkish while still living outwardly in the world. One prays so many times a day, cuts out strong drink, gives alms to the poor, controls one's passions, lives an orderly disciplined and obedient life, studies the scriptures, and avoids occasions of sin, while at the same time working as a craftsman, a banker, a soldier—or, indeed, keeping a home and children. Outwardly, you may seem to be just another ordinary sober citizen of this world. But like a spy you are secretly living a double life, and your true identity will one day be revealed.

This dual way of life—described by Max Weber as "intramundane asceticism"—was classic Christian spirituality, at least for the average lay person living in the world. It was still being punctiliously followed in the nineteenth century by Clapham-Sect Evangelicals, by Methodists, and by Oxford Tractarians. But very much the same spirituality was followed by numbers of Jews and Muslims, and by most Christians until very recently (including me, when younger).

And the point I'm making is now obvious. Classical spiritualities—in Christianity above all, but also in other faiths—were extremely world-denying, and made a sharp distinction between the present very bad outward and passing appearance of things, and the blessed inner and eternal reality of things that would stand forth at the end of time. Christian spirituality to a very high degree attempted to deny this world, and with it the body, the entire secular realm, the passions, sex, and time. It was a way of witnessing to and preparing for the life of a quite different world yet to come—the real life for which we were made, but from which we have been born exiled. It was very long-termist, and was bound up with a large-scale cosmological narrative of Fall and Redemption.

Very fierce asceticism existed until recently. The use of the scourge or discipline, whipping oneself until one drew blood, was practiced by some of the more enthusiastic Puseyites at Oxford in the 1840s, and subsequently, as everyone knows, by William Gladstone. Such people seem to have got from

Italy the implements required, and it is from time to time alleged that there are Catholic circles in which the scourge is still used—as it of course is, in public, in Shia Islam. Very similar oddities are common in the East. But it goes without saying that nobody in the modern West would defend such practices. Among us, a gradual revaluation of everything this-worldly has been going on since the Middle Ages. Step-by-step we revalued the merely-human point of view and the whole human world: human friendship, natural reason, earthly beauty, human love, the body, and so on. But then more recently, human life and the human self have become more and more first enhistorized, and then darwinized. The thorough-going darwinization of human psychology, and even of language and consciousness, is still continuing and it is making the old world-view and the old spirituality simply incomprehensible. Increasingly we have come to believe in only one world, *this* world, as our true home, and so to feel that we need to develop a purely this-worldly understanding, and practice, and justification of religion.

In this context we can now understand why so much of the old vocabulary has become empty and barely usable. The most you can do with it is to create a brief shock-effect by the way you reverse it. Thus the former Roman Catholic priest Charles Davis wrote a book called *Body as Spirit*. Nobody nowadays would wish to commend the sort of flesh-spirit opposition that in the past has alienated people from their own bodiliness. So Davis—like Matthew Fox, who makes many similar moves—declares that bodiliness itself is good and holy. Body is Spirit. But this language both invokes and repudiates the old dualism between body and spirit, and therefore also between outward appearance and inner reality. It's a trick that can be played only once; after that, we have to start changing our vocabulary.

Let me spell this out. As the darwinian revolution comes to permeate the culture more and more deeply, we come to see ourselves in full continuity with the animal background out of which we have evolved. We don't like flesh-spirit dualism any more, and we do not approve of the kind of self-hatred implicit in some traditional ascetical practices. One should not try to crush one's own biological nature. But more than that, we increasingly find repugnant the notion that a religious person is a sort of spy, with a second hidden identity. The Christian, right up to the time of Kierkegaard and even later, was a person who spent her whole life in the closet. You were not to come out until the *parousia*—the moment of final revelation, either in death or at the Second Coming. Until then your spiritual life was a second life, hidden, interior, and secret, that you cultivated assiduously but privately, in preparation for the moment when you would be called out into the open on Judgement Day.

From this it is clear that our dissatisfaction with much traditional spirituality has several related strands. We cannot accept the sort of spirit-flesh dualism that disparages everything fleshly or carnal; and we cannot accept the sort of inner-outer dualism that equates inwardness with reality and outwardness with superficiality, vanity, and "mere" transience. From our twentieth-century point of view, human beings live only one life, and it is a biological life, in only one world, this world; and the movement into outwardness, or "publication," is not a movement *away* from reality but a movement *into* it. That is why, during the nineties, I have been trying to describe an "expressionist" or "solar" kind of spirituality, which sees our religious life in terms of self-expression and coming-out. If we cannot any longer expect to "come out" and to see the Truth manifested in *a future* life, then we must try to bring it all out in the open here and now, in this present life. We live only one life, and it is a *communicative* sort of life, in which we are trying to become ourselves by expressing ourselves. "We live along the wires," and become ourselves in and through our networking with other people. We should be wary nowadays of the ancient tradition that says that we are most ourselves when we are recollected into ourselves in solitude, silence, and inwardness. Isn't the truth rather the opposite of that? Real-ization equals publication. Both Reality and Truth are *processual*, and both require a continual coming-out into the open. Back in the 1840s, Isaac Williams, the author of Tract

80, "On Reserve in Communicating Religious Knowledge" (1842), together with some of his contemporaries revived and applied to the religious life of the individual the ancient idea that one should not speak openly about holy things. They should be kept secret, in the dark. So the modern Christian ought to keep his spiritual life hidden, and not talk about it. John Keble even took the doctrine to the absurd extreme of deliberately preaching boring sermons, in the name of "humility"!

In opposition to that kind of dualism, I am suggesting that we should now simply equate the religious life with our attitude just to life itself, experienced as temporal be-ing. Life pours itself out, spontaneously and ceaselessly, and so should we. The entire religious realm is currently ceasing to be a distinct supernatural world, and is becoming instead something like an imaginative, religious way of construing this life and this world. I still accept the old view that a spirituality is a way of acting out and confirming our picture of the way things are with us human beings, and of the way to happiness. But we are steadily leaving behind us the old contrasts between the earthly world below and the heavenly world above, and between body and soul. We are replacing the old heaven-and-earth world-view with a world-view that knows only "life," or "be-ing." All being is transient or passing. It is a groundless and endless many-stranded outpouring of meaning-events of which our own lives are simply part.

So we are looking for a non-dualistic and "expressive," or "solar," spirituality that does not look to an eternal world above, but goes along with the flux of existence and is content to pour itself out in time along with everyone and everything else. We should not see the religious person as someone who draws back out of life, but rather as someone who plunges recklessly into it, unafraid.

Let's now consider the change in relation to the question of religious happiness. Exactly what is it, and how do we reach it? In the old world-view, religious happiness is to know God and to enjoy him forever in the eternal world. Exactly what the knowledge of God is, and why it makes us happy, is very difficult to say, but it was usually seen as a state of perfect intellectual satisfaction; a complete and intuitive vision of Reality as being necessarily and eternally and perfectly *just so*. Not an easy idea to grasp nowadays; but our present point is that this complete satisfaction couldn't be had in this present world. Christian spirituality was then a discipline in preparation for a better life in a better world that would be fully ours only after death. It follows that the practice of Christianity is justified only if a large-scale story of Fall and Redemption is dogmatically true.

Contrast that traditional long-termism and otherworldliness with the modern position. We are products of the process of *this* world, which is our true and only home. We have only one world, one life, one body. If we still believe that there is such a thing as religious happiness, it's got to be attainable here and now, in the present moment, in time, and in the Fountain, the ceaseless self-renewing flux of events. In this very short-termist set-up, no grand Narrative of otherworldly Redemption is required. The practice of religion is justified insofar, and only insofar, as it promptly delivers the happiness it promises.

But if so, then what *is* religious happiness? In time, language runs unceasingly, and with it the process of the world runs on, both within the self on the near side of language, and out there beyond language in the objective world. Religious language offers us unifying and reconciling symbols through which, from time to time at least, we are able to get ourselves together and to feel ourselves completely in harmony with the world. In such moments we can say Amen to life, and feel completely happy. We are not alienated in any way or from any thing; we are in full continuity with the everlasting flux of things in which we are immersed.

My suggestion is, then, that we are currently changing over from classical spirituality, which was a disciplinary preparation for eternal happiness in another world yet to come, to a new spirituality in which, as we meditate with our eyes open, we are at least sometimes able to find eternal happiness in the present moment. The traditional spirituality was often compared with life under military discipline, or in athletic training. The new spirituality is closer in temper to art.

I should explain this last point further. The old spirituality was predominantly ascetical. One was under discipline, and there was accordingly a strong emphasis upon a large body of religious law, and upon the duty of unconditional obedience to religious authority. The special place given to religious authority and religious law depended upon the claim that the authorities had custody of a body of supremely-important sacred knowledge, upon which everyone's ultimate happiness depended. This knowledge concerned the heavenly world, how we have come to be alienated from it, what remedy is available, and how we can at last be sure of gaining our place in it. So there was the body of divine Truth, there was the religious society, there was authority, law, and all the machinery of salvation. The whole system worked to ensure that you could die happy, fortified by the rites of the church and confident of your place in Heaven.

However, everything depended upon the two-worlds cosmology, and the picture of human beings as amphibians (or perhaps caterpillars, preparing for a more glorious form of life yet to come). When we change over to a one-world and one-life cosmology, everything has to be reassessed. Religious authority, religious law, and the body of divine knowledge all become much less important. Indeed, I now think that religion does not supply us with, nor even depend upon, *any* specially-privileged knowledge that cannot be obtained from other sources. Rather, we should see religion as concerned simply with life itself. We should see prayer and meditation as attention to Being, the continual moment-to-moment forthcoming of everything in time. Being is life's pure givenness, but it comes forth clothed with meanings that we have supplied, as we build our world, interpret our experience, and shape our lives. So religion isn't only a matter of attending to Being; it is also concerned with what we are making of our life, and the meaning that we are giving it. Here we should see religious language and myth as utopian visions, not of a second world to be entered after death, but of a different way this world might be. Religion is halfway between ethics and art; indeed, it is a sort of performance art in which we act out a representation of what our life might be like. Thus the communion service enacts a picture of what community life should be like here and now, and different ways of staging it—that is, technically, different "ceremonies"—elaborate and apply it to different social circumstances.

I'm arguing then that spirituality in future needs to become fully this-worldly and timebound. It will be concerned, not with the things of another world, but with the continual givenness of our this-worldly existence, and what we are making of it. Questions of religious meaning and truth need to be judged, not dogmatically, but pragmatically: religious teachings and practices should be appraised simply in terms of the kind of person and kind of world they tend in practice to produce.

8

The Radical Christian Worldview

SINCE 1960 I have been a priest in the Church of England, and I remain a priest in good standing. But though I still communicate *with* the church, I no longer officiate in the church. Traditionally, a priest has been an institutionally accredited person who purveys a fixed body of knowledge, vocabulary, and set of rituals, and it is no longer in me to be such a person. I love freedom too much. I have spent almost all my career teaching the philosophy of religion and writing, and have come to think that none of our religious traditions can survive as it stands. All of them need reform, and the mainstream Christian tradition in particular—Orthodox, Catholic, and Protestant—urgently needs revolutionary transformation. Since the Enlightenment and the rise of critical thinking, it has become almost a cliché that the church's world-view is long obsolete, that the doctrine-system is very wrong, and that the church's hierarchical pattern of government encourages vanity and inhibits change. In effect, each of the old men says to himself: "No, not in my time: the *status quo* will see me out"—and he does nothing. So by small increments the situation has been allowed to grow steadily worse, to the point where it may already be too late to hope for reform and renewal.

From the church's point of view I am only a marginal Christian now: I am someone who likes modern Western philosophy, who retains a strong devotion to Jesus Christ, who has an affinity with much in the Jewish and the Buddhist traditions, and who has been trying to build up a body of free and experimental religious writing which may or may not one day be of use to others.[1]

In light of this understanding of who I am, I have been asked a number of questions that I will address in this essay.

WHAT IS YOUR CONCEPTION OF GOD OR THE ULTIMATE?

There is no Ultimate: everything is proximate. There is no Absolute: everything is relative. There is nothing primary and founding: everything is secondary. The human world around us is not beneath and subordinate to a Higher World above, because, on the contrary, "Nothing is hidden," and all this is all there is. The human world—that is, the world as it is for *us*—is now effectively the *only* world, because we are, it seems, the only beings who have a complete world. There is no other world but ours. The human world is outsideless, and is coextensive with the range of our language—which is finite but now very large. It includes the whole known universe and all that is known of human history.

Traditional Jewish, Christian, and Muslim ideas of God have been heavily dependent upon Greek philosophy, which was strongly realistic. The world was seen as preceding us: it was a readymade cosmos, created by the imposition of form upon matter, law upon disorder, and intelligible meaning upon the sensuous flux. The Greeks saw these rational principles, by which the raw stuff of the world has been made a Cosmos, as really existing out there in an objective Order of Reason, and ultimately in the Divine Mind. The Greeks thus grounded everything normative, and the whole world order, in mind stuff out there. Their thinking was highly objectivist, and their philosophy gravitated steadily toward realistic meta-

---

[1] The ideas presented in this essay are developed in more detail in the following recent books: *After All* (1994), *The Last Philosophy* (1995), *Solar Ethics* (1995), *After God* (1997), *Mysticism after Modernity* (1997), *The Religion of Being* (1998), *The Revelation of Being* (1998), *The New Religion of Life in Everyday Speech* (1999), and *The Meaning of It All in Everyday Speech* (1999).

physical theism. Recent ideas about just when the books of the Hebrew Bible were written and compiled suggest that the most developed and universalistic ideas about God in the Old Testament (to be found in Isaiah, chapters 40–55) were already strongly influenced by Greek thought.[2] Thus religious belief in God has since early times been locked into an important Greek philosophical doctrine—metaphysical realism. This doctrine pictures our thinking and our rationality as derived from and dependent upon an objective Logos that pervades the cosmos. Before we were, it was already out there. When we think aright, our thinking participates in and tracks the cosmic Divine Mind. To think Newtonian physics, for example, was to think God's thoughts after him—something that indeed we had been created by God to do, for it was believed that "Man" had been specially created by God to be his vicegerent upon earth.

Thus belief in God was tied to an unhistorical and supernaturalist view of reason, and to a very exalted view of "Man" as the crown of creation. It was sincerely believed that the human being (or, to be a little more explicit, the male human mind) was a finite copy of the infinite Divine Mind, and that the concepts through which we think are little copies of the unchanging Divine Ideas. God came first: God made the world to be a house for us to live in, and then made us with minds like God's, so that we would know how to live in it.

I don't want to retell here the story of how these ways of thinking died, and died finally in the nineteenth century. I need only say that fully orthodox realistic metaphysical belief in God has for a long time been quite impossible for an educated Westerner. We have come to see ourselves as products of an evolutionary process that has, and *has* to have, a lot of random in it and therefore *cannot* be God-directed. We have to come to see that we ourselves have evolved all our own languages, knowledge-systems, and visions of the world. Our

---

[2] See the reconstructed history of ancient Israel in Thomas L. Thompson, *The Bible in History: How Writers Create a Past* (London: Jonathan Cape, 1999).

religions, too, exactly like all our other social institutions, are now seen as humanly evolved products of history. That is how they are treated in textbooks of "comparative religion," and that is how we know it is. *We* invented all the rational principles, all the world-views, and all the religions.

But if all this has happened, what does a person like me do about belief in God? I find that as the old metaphysical idea of God has disintegrated, God-talk and religious feeling have become scattered and splashed over a variety of different aspects of our human life and experience. Instead of the old sort of dialogue-prayer, I practice "the mysticism of secondariness" and "moving-edge meditation." God becomes *an ideal standard of perfection* by which I judge myself and am judged. God is the divinity of *Love*, which above all else makes our life worth living. Commitment to God becomes resolved into commitment to and belief in *life*. The practice of the presence of God becomes attention to *Be-ing*. The old burning zeal has become what I call *solar ethics*.

I am a post-dogmatic believer. None of the old dogmas are true any more. The old realistic metaphysics of God is dead, and I certainly do not believe in *that* God any longer. Nobody can, any more. But the death of God has in effect *scattered* the divine across the human life-world, sacralizing many aspects of our experience. I have gained more than I have lost, because I now find the Holy in all that was once thought to be *merely* human, *merely* relative, and (above all) *merely* transient. The death of God makes *everything* holy.

People who are in love with absolute monarchy will naturally regard the radical Christian point of view as "atheism." But that label is too crudely political. The old belief in God was highly authoritarian: it saw religion simply in terms of absolute monarchy, and thought that the only alternative to absolute monarchy must be pure anarchy. But the radical Christian is a religious democrat for whom sovereignty is now dispersed across the whole body politic. I like religious immanence, and a widely scattered sacred. It makes possible a much more varied and richer piety, and it is quite free from the hysterical absolutism of the orthodox.

IN WHAT WAYS DOES YOUR UNDERSTANDING OF RELIGION
OFFER A MEANS OF HUMAN LIBERATION?

Most of the world's major religious traditions developed during the Iron Age. Karl Jaspers dated what he called "the Axial Period" from 800 B.C.E. to 200 C.E.[3] Others may prefer to move the dates a few centuries later, but there is no great disagreement about the magnitude of the cultural changes that were taking place at that time. It was the period of the rise of philosophy and of the first attempts at systematic scientific and historical enquiry. It was the period of the first large empires, bringing conditions in which creative individuals could travel, write, speculate, teach, and attract disciples, and experiment with new lifestyles such as those of the monk and the wandering philosopher.

Against this background, the emergent world religions naturally took the form of mass movements inspired by the teaching and example of a venerated founder. They were usually ascetical "ways" or "paths," by following which one could hope gradually to be liberated from all that is wrong with human nature and the human condition. And they were usually *dualistic,* making a clear contrast between the present unsatisfactory world of fleeting images, half-truths, and disorderly passions, and an unchanging Better World of absolute contemplative knowledge and unalloyed bliss which was the goal of the religious quest.

There is a certain tendency nowadays to see religious doctrine-systems as picturesque and popular versions of systems of philosophy, or even as primitive scientific theories. But if the great Iron Age religions first arose as communal pathways to individual salvation, it is surely better to see their doctrine-systems as guides or handbooks for the traveler on the Way.

Now the question arises: Should religion today still be taking the form of a path to individual redemption or salvation?

I answer: With qualifications, yes. But the qualifications are

---

[3] Karl Jaspers, *The Origin and Goal of History* (London: Routledge and Kegan Paul, 1953).

very substantial, because for some time now it has been very
obvious that both monasticism and the two-worlds picture of
reality that goes with it have come to an end. There is only
one world, this world, the human life-world, and there is no
sense in the idea that we might come to live under wholly
different conditions of existence, perhaps in another world altogether, while yet still being ourselves. But though our view
of things is now naturalistic, it is not passive and quietistic.
Radical Christians follow prophets like Nietzsche and D. H.
Lawrence in believing that human life, human nature, and the
human world are not what they might be. We do believe that
individual human beings and the whole human world could
be very much better and happier than they now are, and we
seek to offer a new understanding of self, selves, and world in
which one can find complete happiness. But we do *not* offer
any sort of disciplinary doctrine-system or new creed. The religious society used to be compared with a ship's crew, a
school, or an army on the march. It was seen as needing to
have a clearly defined system of discipline and chain of command. But radical Christians reject the "orthodoxy" in which
truth is controlled by power, and dislike the mental numbness
induced by canonical forms of words. In our view, religious
truth cannot be canonized in fixed doctrines or forms of words.
It needs to be continually reminted by the invention of new
metaphors. So we see religious liberation as very often taking
the form of liberation from the tyranny of religion that has
become old, objectified, oppressive, and ugly. And although
we do not look to any other world, we do look for a big change
in the way we see our life in *this* world.

Radical Christianity is in my view a form of radical humanism, in which we find eternal happiness in being wholly given
over to our world, which for its part is also wholly given to
us. To say a wholehearted Yes to one's own, and the world's,
lightness and transience is bliss. I have sometimes called this
idea "energetic Spinozism," but it is much misunderstood,
and here I shall explain it by briefly arguing that it is the cul-
mination of the history of religion.

Suppose we consider the questions: What is all this? What

determines the way things go in it all? Who's running every-thing? Can we humans ever learn to influence it or them? In the earliest world-views that we can hope to describe, reality was seen as a scrum, a ceaseless conflict of terrifying Powers who were of course entirely absorbed in their wrestling with each other and utterly indifferent to the helpless human spec-tator. There was no "matter;" there were only the Powers. There was no unified human subject, because the conflict of the Powers reached deep into the region where we would now put human subjectivity. Human beings had very little knowl-edge of or control over nature, and human subjectivity was relatively undeveloped. The Powers raged as violently within us as they did around us.

Here in this most archaic of all world-views, reality is seen at its most objective, sacred, violent, and disorganized. Thus described, it gives us a clue to the direction that the long struggle for human liberation must take. Religious ideology and religious practice must, *first*, over the long millennia grad-ually get the objective world organized and unified, for exam-ple by gradually moving from animism to polytheism, to henotheism and monotheism and then to naturalism. And then, *secondly*, they must also get the subjective world orga-nized, for example by pulling the self back from the world and drawing a line between subjectivity and objectivity; and then by a long ascetical struggle, gradually making the self more calm, unified, and controlled. And, *thirdly*, religion also needs ways of building up the strength of the human subject, so that there can be a better balance of power between subjectivity and objectivity. A Prometheus is needed, who will steal tech-nical power from the divine world and give it to humans; a Moses, who by giving the divine Law to humans will help to persuade humans that they, too, can exercise legislative and world-ordering power and authority; and a Christ, who will bring pure Deity into the life of ordinary humanity.

In the beginning, humans were extremely weak and vulner-able. They were at the mercy of warring Powers of which they had almost no understanding or control. Only very gradually did they manage to gain some degree of technical control—for example, over fire—and then later, by domestication, over some species of animals and plants. With that technical control came a growing ability to recognize regularities and causal connections in the skies and on earth. Gradually, we built up our own increasingly large-scale and complex world-picture— a world-picture from which the old Powers had vanished. Gradually, the old realism died as we came to recognize that our world—the complex world-picture that *we* had built up, the *known* world, which is to say, the world in our knowledge—is in effect *the* world. We are not in any position to compare the world in our knowledge with the world as it exists out there and independently of our knowledge. And what is more, we are the only beings who have a complete world-picture, in which everything is by now theorized.

So our world has been comprehensively delivered to us and belongs to us. Apart from us, there is nothing but the ultralight flux of transient Be-ing. There is no *rival* to us, or threat to us, out there: it is all ours.

The sort of religious liberation that is available to us in our post-modern times combines anti-realism with radical humanism. It has been made accessible to us by the growing completeness of our theory. Knowledge has developed so far and so fast that we have thoroughly theorized almost everything around us, *and within* us, too. We, too, are our own constructs. Everywhere we look we see a world that is *already* humanly appropriated, theorized, historized, and interpreted. Nothing quite nonhuman remains except the gentle forthcoming of Be-ing, which is everything's utter contingency. It is a bit like Heaven, or "the Kingdom of God"—but temporalized and without the gold. "Solar ethics" is, all the time, to choose it as bliss. And it is, I say, a kind of fulfillment of the history of religion. Yes: we are at the end of history.

HOW DOES YOUR CONCEPTION OF RELIGION DEAL WITH THE PROBLEM OF EVIL?

The question about evil (*unde malum:* whence is evil?) is formulated variously in different religious traditions around the world, but I suggest that in this present context the problem is one of disappointed expectations. Orthodox theism says that nothing happens by chance: every event is willed by Almighty God, and plays its part in the fulfillment of his ethical purpose. This belief gives rise to a presumption that all the world will turn out to be governed like a state ruled by a very wise and powerful king who watches over his subjects and arranges for everyone to get their deserts, the virtuous being rewarded with prosperity and happiness and the wicked being duly punished. Then people ask: Why are things not as we felt entitled to expect? Why is there so much evil in the world? Why is there *metaphysical evil*—finitude, transience, and death? Why is there so much *moral evil*—human wickedness, much of it going apparently unpunished? Why is there so much *physical evil*—innocent and undeserved suffering (including perhaps animal suffering)?

Why do bad things happen to good people? asked a popular U.S. bestseller a few years ago—the general presumption being that bad things surely ought never to happen to good people like us. *Why is it all so unfair?* people ask, their presumption being that they were *entitled* to expect life to be fair. They thought that the world would turn out to be like a well-run school, with an unseen Fatherly Eye watching over everyone's conduct and handing out rewards and punishments accordingly. When they discover that the world is not governed like an idealized patriarchal household, they are extremely shocked and distressed.

One may well wonder why people have such bizarre expectations. The answer is surely that people have always got their first idea of God and the way God runs things in their childhood, when their parents and other teachers were endeavoring to impress upon them the importance of morality. So they were taught to see the world as being like a big family, presided over by a stern but wise and loving father; or like a boarding school run by a strict but fair Headmaster; or like a storybook kingdom ruled by a good and wise king. To a much larger degree than we care to admit, our religious ideas reflect a childhood vision of the world.

So I simply refuse "the problem of evil" as it is usually presented. Orthodox belief in a good and almighty God pictures the world as a cosmos, completely determinate and with all events predestined. But it now appears that at the micro level the world-process is indeterminate and random. Exactly which atom will decay next, which person will be the next to contract meningitis, and which mutation will occur next cannot be predicted. Large-scale outcomes can often be predicted, but at the micro level, the world is simply *not* the fully determined cosmos that realistic theists believe in, and there *is not* the objective moral providence that they used to believe in.[4] Today, surely, nobody seriously suggests that moral considerations help to determine just who is going to have an accident or fall ill. It seems that there is not an objective moral providence, and that the process of the world is simply contingent. Only human beings are wise or unwise, and moral or immoral. By the arrangements we make we can reduce our own statistical liability to suffer various sorts of misfortune, and by the moral institutions we establish we can make things better or worse for other people and for ourselves. But the world as such and apart from us is unformed and innocent. Since commitment to God is commitment to the values of justice and love, belief in God may and should inspire people to try to make the world a better place, but it does not—and it never did—offer any kind of magical protection against life's sheer contingency.

You may say that my refusal of the standard "problem of evil" is unwarrantedly optimistic and "fails to take evil really seriously"—as if it were true that nothing is being taken seriously unless it is being reified, a proposition that might lead to some very odd conclusions. I reply that my own ideas about evil, suffering, and death were formed at a time when I was myself *in extremis*. Solar living, on the basis of a full acceptance of contingency, of our own vulnerability and mortality—and

---

[4] I make the distinction here because today there are professed realistic theists, such as John Hick, who have in effect given up the personality of God and his all-determining moral Providence.

acceptance, too, of certain well-known facts about human beings—is the only effective "answer" to evil. Nothing else
works.

What we have to do is to give up "realism"—that is, give
up the belief in substances, including the belief that we are or
have "immortal souls." So long as we think that a bit of us is
not of this world and has to be preserved unsullied for another
life elsewhere, we will fail to commit ourselves completely to
this world and this life. Instead we need to recognize that
there is only the language-formed flux that appears objectively
as the world and subjectively as the self. We'll slowly begin to
see that the world is all ours, and that we wholly belong to
our world. In that complete unity of self and world lies the
possibility of solar living and our eternal happiness. Practice it
by practicing any activity (philosophy, meditation, craftwork,
or whatever) that enables you to become fully absorbed and
taken right out of yourself. Learn to live like that all the time
and you will be learning solar living, a way of living that for-
gets the past and the future and that simply burns, now.

Do you believe in any form of the Afterlife?

The parameters for the answer to this question have already
been set out. First, there is only one world, the human world,
the life-world. The belief in a higher, eternal World Above
can be seen finally fading out of Western thought in the philosophy of Kant. Since his time, no thinker of note has been
able to do anything to make "life after death," as popularly
understood, either credible or even intelligible. The desire to
believe in life after death has remained so strong that even
some first-rate minds—among them Kant himself—have been
willing to consider the alleged evidence from spiritualism and
"psychical research." But for two hundred years it has been
getting less and less possible to revive belief in life after
death, as we have more and more come to see how profoundly
every aspect of our being is interwoven with this world of ours.

Every last bit of us is *situated* in the here and now, biologically, historically, and culturally. We are not detachable from our world, and it comes as no surprise that those contemporary novelists who have wished to use the idea of heaven have been obliged to picture it as being simply a fantasy-continuation of this life.[5]

However, and secondly, I have long argued that "Christian life is life after life after death."[6] That is to say: when we abandon the popular notion of life after death, it becomes possible for us to understand the *Christian* idea of life after death. From the earliest times, entry into Christianity was by undergoing ritual death and rebirth in union with Christ, so that the Christian's entire life thenceforth was supposed to be a "risen," postmortem life. Liberated from fear, greed, and attachment, the believer lived a dying life—like the sun, whose life is renewed all the time by the same thermonuclear process that keeps it dying all the time.

To live in this way is to live on the basis of complete acceptance of one's own, and everything else's, contingency and transience. One finds eternal happiness in being fully merged into "the Fountain," the continual pouring-out and passing-away of everything.

People influenced by classical metaphysics see the transient world of Becoming as resting upon and supported by an unseen world of eternal Being. Religious existence is a matter of resting upon a rock. But in my account, religious existence is a matter of resting like a ping-pong ball upon a fountain—or perhaps rather, of simply going along with and accepting the flux of contingency of which one is a part.[7] Is it not exactly this mysticism of contingency, or secondariness, that everyone recognizes and loves so much in the later painting of Claude Monet?

---

[5] See novels by Michael Frayn and Julian Barnes for heaven as a bourgeois fantasy version of the good life.

[6] From *The Sea of Faith* (1984).

[7] The artist Damien Hirst has a work in which a ping-pong ball is supported on the rising column of air from a tilted-back hairdryer.

IN WHAT RESPECTS IS YOUR OWN RELIGIOUS POSITION DIFFERENT FROM THE MAINSTREAM TRADITION?

In order to answer this question accurately I have to make a distinction between two kinds of Christianity: Church Christianity and Kingdom Christianity.

According to a well-known saying, "Jesus preached the Kingdom—but it was the Church that came." This is comparable with: "Karl Marx taught communism—but what we got was Marxism-Leninism-Stalinism and the dictatorship of the proletariat." The fiercely oppressive Soviet system was supposed to be only a stopgap for the interim period during which the old bad ways were being abolished and the new kind of man was being bred. But as time went on, the withering-away of the state began to look less and less likely. The apparatchiks were enjoying their privileges and their security too much, and had no interest in planning their own obsolescence as a class. So the dictatorship of the proletariat in the socialist state became, in effect, an end in itself, and the fully communist society was postponed indefinitely.

The same thing happened in Christianity. Within the Jewish tradition the distinction between the present state of religious mediation and the final state of simple, humanistic religious immediacy was well established. In the present order, the believer's access to God was mediated by written scriptures, the Temple, the sacrificial system, and various religious professionals. God was portrayed as a remote objective being, a distant king and judge. But one day things would improve. In the age to come religious objectification would end: the Law would come to be written on each believer's heart. God would cease to be an objective being, and instead would be distributed into each believer's heart as Spirit. People would no longer be dominated by religious professionals. Religion would become fully democratized.

Jesus proclaimed the coming of such an era, calling it "the Kingdom of God." But in the writing of the most important of his early followers, Paul, we already see the beginnings of a relapse into mediated religion.[8] Paul wants power and control over the people he writes to, and, above all, he wants control of *truth*. By the mid-second century, the male clergy were seizing power over almost every aspect of church life, and they created Christian doctrine as an ideology of the kind of mediated religion from which they derived their own status and power. Jesus, who had been the enemy of mediated religion, now himself became the Mediator. The Kingdom was pushed away into the heavenly world beyond death, with the clergy having the keys to it. This meant that there was no longer any danger of the clergy's being made redundant by the arrival of the Kingdom on earth. Henceforth, anyone who taught the possibility of immediate religion could be described as a "gnostic," a "mystic," a "heretic," or whatever, and duly persecuted. The kind of religion that Jesus came to preach was abolished in his name, being replaced by a curious idolatry of the church and of the spiritual power that had come to be vested in the higher clergy. In time, people completely forgot the idea that what is called "orthodox Christian doctrine" was merely a way of thinking appropriate for a transitional period of training or discipline, when people were under authority, and that it existed in a state of ardent longing for its own supersession by something much better. Instead, people honestly began to think that church doctrine was *the Truth*, forever.

It isn't. It served well enough in premodern times, but with the rise of modern science and critical thinking, as well as the rise of democratic politics and humanitarianism, it has become hopelessly out of date. We now urgently need to make the move away from the old cruelly authoritarian Church Christianity to a new this-worldly and democratic Christian humanism. One religious group, the Quakers, made the shift over three centuries ago, and their example gives a rough idea of what might be involved.

I can now answer the question about my relation to the "mainstream tradition." Those who think that Church Christianity is the final form of Christianity will obviously regard

---

[8] Graham Shaw, *The Cost of Authority* (London: SCM Press, 1983).

me as being no longer a Christian. I reply that they have forgotten their own theology and have made an idol of the
church-system and its ideology.

Having defined a radical Christian as a Christian who thinks
that the church has completed its historical mission, and that
we now need to make the move to the final state of religion
whose "nearness" Jesus originally preached, I end by noting
the close similarity between the radical Christian world-view
and the world-view of post-modern philosophy. Perhaps post-
modernity is itself Christianity's final expression, now coming
into being. In summary:

1. Everything is transient, everything is contingent, everything
    just pours out and passes away.
2. Reality is a ceaseless flux of communication.
3. On its inner surface, the flux resolves itself into a network
    of persons, who include you and me: on its outer surface,
    the flux is "screened" as the objective world, the life-world,
    the world of experience.
4. The divine is the light that irradiates everything; it is every-
    thing's be-ing, intelligibility, and bliss.

This picture of a world that has become all communication,
and that is radically humanist, derives from familiar biblical
texts such as Revelation 21 and Jeremiah 31:31–34. And it is
the world-picture of post-modern, post-historical philosophy.
The time has come: we should seize the day.

4

The Turn to Life

9

The Value of Life

WHAT SORT OF ETHIC are we going to need in a world that is becoming increasingly environmentally-conscious?

Just to ask this question is to show what a long way we have come, for it suggests that we do now, at last, admit that moralities are purely human productions, evolved by human societies, and quite properly responsive to local and occasional needs. The figures and the forecasts that we are getting from the scientists seem to be telling us that if we want to survive we must hasten to design ourselves some new values and start living by them. And this is at first sight very paradoxical and post-modern, for on the one hand, it indicates that everything is invented and all our highest and most precious beliefs and values are mere cultural fictions, while on the other hand, it simultaneously urges the necessity of devising authoritative new beliefs and values that will more strictly control our economic activities than ever the sincerely-held dogmatic religion of the past succeeded in doing.

That is a strange requirement, but the paradox is not easily avoided. There are people who claim that the remedy for our present troubles lies in a return to a rather traditional version of the doctrine of creation. But such a willed revival of lost belief is even more fictitious than the creation of new values. How do you go back before Darwinism, before modern physics and cosmology, and before "chaos science" and our recent recognition of the systematic unpredictability and fragility of much in nature? The revivalists are asking for a restoration of something like eighteenth-century "Designer Realism," with its reassuringly stable and balanced vision of nature as a benevolently planned and smoothly running machine—in short, a real Cosmos. But recent scientific development cannot be revoked at will. In any case, although the pioneers of the in-

dustrial revolution were sincere Protestant believers, there is
no evidence that any of them, before sinking a mineshaft or
opening a smelting works, spent much time asking himself
whether these industrial activities might have adverse effects
upon the divinely-established natural order. If Christian doctrine did not successfully dissuade people in the past, is it
likely to become more effective in the future? And if in the
past even divine Truth, wholeheartedly believed, had only the
most marginal influence upon people's economic activities,
how are acknowledged fictions going to fare any better? Furthermore, a regress threatens us, for what values are to guide
our making and choosing of new values?

The paradox, then, is that in an age more profoundly skeptical and, indeed, nihilistic than ever before, we are faced with
the task of fictioning for ourselves a new and authoritative
value system and view of the world whose influence upon our
conduct will cut deeper than that of religion used to do.
Deeper, because this time the focus of our "ultimate concern"
falls upon the natural world, the most basic economic activities, and biological life. This time we are thinking of religion
as concerned, not just with redeeming or supplementing or
transforming nature, but with the very survival of natural life.
In the past, the great religions were able to take straightforward biological life more-or-less for granted. Indeed, they relatively devalued it, as being part of our "lower nature" that we
shared with mere animals and plants. The important thing was
not "merely" to live, like a beast, but to live *well,* and indeed
to leave natural human life altogether behind in favor of eternal life and immortality. Our forebears were spared the knowledge that one day mother's milk might become unfit to drink.
When that day comes we are forced to see life itself as a value,
and perhaps the first value. At any rate, it is the precondition
for the attainment of any other value. So when our practical
thoughtlessness has brought us to the brink of self-destruc-
tion, we have to ask ourselves whether life itself matters to us.
Do we want the human enterprise to continue? What *is* "life,"
and why should it be valued? Thus our nihilism confronts us
with a highly metaphysical question. Not quite the classical

question, Why is there something rather than nothing? To that there is an obvious retort: why *shouldn't* there be something rather than nothing? We have no reason to think that there-being-nothing is or was the prior, the simpler, and the more intelligible state of affairs. Rather the opposite, as Bergson pointed out. But our present question is different. It is the more existential question: Why should we wish to live rather than not live? Why do we want earthly life to go on, and what makes life a value? What is the *value* of our values that makes us want to go on living and striving to realize them? We are reminded here of the solemn debates about suicide of Camus and Sartre in the 1940s. For twentieth-century thinkers life itself is an issue. We can no longer assume that life will continue unproblematically, providing us with the unregarded substrate upon which we build our ethical and religious structures. When the very survival of life itself is in question, then the cultural superstructure of morality, religion, politics, and so on has to turn back and address itself to the problem of its own base. As has happened in modern philosophy, the whole distinction between base and superstructure then breaks down.

It is worth dwelling on this point for a moment. Especially in the English-speaking world, a long tradition inclines us to believe that there is a level of objective facts out there prior to interpretation, that there is nature out there prior to culture, and that there is matter out there prior to and independent of the world of signs. However, in philosophy there are well-known reasons for holding that we have no access to any sheerly-given and uninterpreted level of bare fact. Everything that we lay hold of we have thereby already interpreted. Facts emerge only within schemes of interpretation, scientific and other ideas about nature emerge only within culture, and theories of matter or whatever else is supposed to be original or basic in the world emerge only within the realm of language. Thus we increasingly see the ideological superstructure as being a Derridean "supplement," curving back to become responsible for the structuring of its own base; and modern environmentalism may be seen as a practical and everyday version

of the same point. Nature isn't something wild, extra-cultural
and out there, from which we distance ourselves and which
we set out to conquer. On the contrary, it is increasingly our
product and a reflection of ourselves; we are responsible for it
and must look after it.

As for the notion that we must now invent and establish
new values, that is not so novel as it may seem. Since the
Enlightenment it has become clear to us human beings that
we make culture, we make language, and we make our own
history. We are therefore responsible not only for living up to
our beliefs and our values, but also for the beliefs and values
themselves. Knowledge doesn't drop from Heaven any more;
we make it, for our own purposes. And the values of things
are not fixed eternally and unchangeably any longer; they are
socially established, and can be changed by social action. The
moral task is therefore to respond to historical change by
bringing about appropriate social, moral, and political changes.
We need to revise current valuations, and, if need be, to establish entirely new values. The way this is done is by the now-
very-familiar method of forming a pressure group and campaigning for the public recognition and legal entrenchment of
new rights. And in fact the moral history of the West since the
1780s has largely consisted in the activities of innumerable
campaigning pressure groups. These groups have had the
imagination and the wit to recognize social evils, to invent
new rights, and to single out new topics of moral concern.
Theory has been slow to admit it, but in fact we have been
moral anti-realists or creationists for two centuries; that is, our
moral tradition has grown and developed by the continuing
invention and social entrenchment of new values. We have
had difficulty in recognizing this, because ideologically we
have mostly been committed to moral realism. That is, we
have wanted to believe in real moral standards, essences, values—in short, "absolutes"—subsisting timelessly out there
and apart from us. So we have tended to overlook or deny the
extent to which we ourselves invent morality and initiate
moral change. However, anyone nowadays who has had some
decades of adult life has personally experienced the process

of adjusting to profoundly changing moral values. We have experienced the arrival of environmentalism, sexism, racism, and so on. These words, and the new valuations that they have brought with them, have become built into our speech habits and are changing the way we live. Massive moral change has occurred in our own time, and therefore can occur. *It happens*, and therefore the invention of new and authoritative values in response to the environmental crisis cannot be as paradoxical an idea as it at first seems to us.

I am suggesting, therefore, that in our quest for a satisfactory environmentalist ethic the first requirement is that we shall acknowledge that our *de facto* ethic is already one of value-creation. If we can but get rid of the old realistic illusions about absolute or objective truth and value, and acknowledge instead that truth-production and value-production are continuous, ever-renewed, creative human activities, then we will be able to square up to the task of creating an environmentalist ethic. Yes, the question of life is now a theological question; it has that sort of depth and ultimacy. And yes, in principle we must be able to invent an answer to it. In both religion and morality, the anti-realist point of view makes solutions possible because it allows us to be creative in good conscience.

Earlier moralities are now mostly unsuitable. They very often began from the is-ought distinction. That is, they drew a clear contrast between the realm of what is and the realm of what ought to be, between the actual and the ideal, between the indicative and the imperative. So the very first move in morality was one that downgraded the actual relative to the moral ideal. We were taught to be dissatisfied with things as they are, and to lift up our eyes toward the ideal world of things as they should be. Everything natural, changeable, sensuous, passionate, and fleeting, that is, everything *alive* was "merely" profane, low-grade in comparison. A series of hierarchies was established that ranked the human higher than the animal and the vegetable, reason higher than the passions and the flesh, duty higher than inclination, the universal higher than the particular, and so on, all of which had the effect of pushing life's center of gravity out of life, and creating a great stronghold of controlling value-power in a more spiritual world beyond this world. The ethical was thus set up as a quasi-masculine command, rational, universal, and unchanging, that emanated from a superior realm beyond life.

We are still very deeply influenced by these ancient ideas. The dualisms of is and ought, flesh and spirit, inclination and reason leave behind them a persisting suspicion that an ethic that affirms the sensuous is "merely" aesthetic (i.e., not truly moral at all), and that an ethic that affirms the actual must be quietistic. It is no accident that even to this day, "moralism" signifies a domineering discontent and disapprobation of the way things are. And by the same token, there is evidently a close relationship between environmentalism, feminism, and attempts to criticize and escape from the old masculinist dualisms with which our culture was first built.

What then might a truly environmentalist ethical theory, consistent with all the points I have been making, look like? I have rejected the is-ought distinction because it separates the world of the moral ideal from the life-world. I have rejected moral realism with its so-called "absolutes" because, again, it seeks to present the moral realm as being sovereign, extra-human, extra-historical, and unchanging. I have also rejected the idea that there is any non-moral world of material and value-neutral fact. So, we see no reason to think of morality either as having to be pushed up into an ideal world above, or as having to be pushed into the sphere of human subjectivity. Instead, our morality is to be simply a morality of life, and the moral world is the life-world. The good is equated with life's endless productivity and joy in itself.

What then is life? We see the world as being something like a communications network, with messages flying back and forth in all directions all the time. Life is the quivering, pulsating energy that carries the messages. So the minimum unit of which the world is made is some little vibration or wavelet, a difference, a minute packet of energy. Think of it as a flicker in your own sensibility, as you feel a little pulse of sensation or emotion. The flicker is a flicker of *life*. It is always felt evaluatively as being pleasurable or painful, turning us on or turning us off, likeable or dislikeable; and culture may encode it as a word. For culture works by training and calibrating our biological sensibility so that quivers in it are felt as evaluations, expressed as feelings, and read as meanings.

Thus the world has two faces or aspects, roughly corresponding to the distinction between the science and the arts subjects. On one face, the world is a flux of minute events, and a process of energy-exchange. On its other face, the world is a world of language, a sea of meanings. These two faces of the world are as close to each other as the two sides of a sheet of paper.

A culture, then, may be defined as a complex evaluation and interpretation of life in which each member of society gets trained from the earliest infancy. As a result of this training, every pulse in our sensibility gets a valuation annexed to it which enables it to be read as a meaning. Culture teaches us, that is, a very complex differential valuation of life that structures the world and makes it intelligible. Valuation makes knowledge possible, in that it is only because we have an *interest* in life that we can know things.

Obviously, culture must train us in a sufficiently high overall valuation of life to make us feel that, taking all things together, life is indeed worth living. But there are considerable variations between cultures, some being more optimistic and others more pessimistic. In the more optimistic cultures, there is a relatively higher overall valuation of everything and therefore more *joie de vivre*. But valuation creates reality: that is, when we are depressed and we value ourselves and our world very low, then everything is gray and unreal; whereas when our enjoyment of life is at its highest, the world is at its most real, solid and brightly-colored. So the value of life is not a fixed and objective quantity but depends upon culture. Our current valuation of life is publicly visible in our linguistic usages. The way we speak of things shows how we value them.

Now culture can change, linguistic usages can change, and valuations can change. Life can therefore be revalued. I am suggesting that it is rational for us to adopt that ethic that, taken all together, is the most life-enhancing because it gives rise to the highest overall valuation, of every bit of our world and of our life-experience, that is self-consistently possible. The best ethic is the one that makes life fullest, in every respect.

There is no sense in the foundationalist idea that we could make an entirely fresh start in morality. On the contrary, if we are human then we are always already within a culture; that is, within a complex historically-evolved evaluation of life. But there is a case for moral change if we find that our culture's present overall evaluation of life is not as high as it might be. Perhaps there are aspects of our life, or feelings, or classes of people, or animals, or bits of the environment that could be more highly valued. In that case, if these things can be upgraded, life will be enriched for everyone.

How is this revaluation to be accomplished? Since our present culturally prescribed valuation of life is carried in the language, our vocabulary itself shows us very clearly who currently has a dirty name and is therefore a *prima facie* candidate for upgrading. A simple example is the snake. As everyone knows, very ancient cultural traditions have left these beautiful and highly-evolved animals with a very bad name. In many parts of the world they are treated atrociously. To survive they must be given a better name, or, as it is often put nowadays, a better image, and then they may begin to be treated better. So, in the modern period, moral change is very commonly initiated by single-issue pressure groups that nag away at language. They try to persuade us to look more critically at usages such as those that associate the black with the sinister, that make woman always come second to man, that make the poor less "noble" and of "lower" "quality" than the rich, and that make the gay person a "pervert." If we can become more critical of such habitual and unnecessarily negative evaluations, we may be able to change them in a way that will make the world a better place for everyone.

This sketch of an environmentalist moral theory attempts to reconcile three different interests. On the one hand, any environmental ethic has clearly got to be naturalistic. That is to say, it must be an ethic of life and feeling. It must not devalue the near-at-hand by projecting its standards of moral perfection out into an ideal world above. It must find the highest value in the here-and-now.

However, and in the second place, our environmental ethic must not fall into the old errors of natural law theory. We have no access to any unchanging natures of things independent of language and history and culture. Life, nature, world-picture, and moral values are all of them constructed within the world of language and culture and historical change. Only if we consistently maintain this can we avoid the illusions (and, too often, the self-interestedness) of conservationism. There is no extra-historical state of nature to be gone back to, or to be conserved. To put it in simple everyday terms, landscapes are just as much historically-produced as are townscapes, and nature is as much a human construct as culture. Environmentalism itself must be constructive and not conservative.

So, thirdly, on our account, the very notion of a stable ethic and value-system disappears. It is replaced by a new conception of the moral life as a continually-changing, innovative, and productive activity. We are always already in a tradition. Our task is always to appraise it, criticize it, reinterpret it, develop it, *add* to it. Values, like truths, need constantly to be refurbished. Morality lives by continually discovering new causes of moral concern. We have to keep on postulating new human rights and striving to entrench them.

Clearly we cannot speak of progress in the sense of steadily-closer approximation to some timeless standard of perfection, for we have no access to any such standard. Nor can we speak of progress in the sense of drawing closer to the Goal of history. Alas, nothing guarantees either the conservation of values or the compossibility of all positive values, and experience suggests that as we create new values, old ones are always slipping away and being lost. However, we do dare to speak of progress in the more limited and restricted sense that there are many, many areas of our experiences, classes of people, and features of our environment that could be loved and appreciated more than they at present are. It is, we claim, possible to enhance the value of life: so we should try to do it. It is rational so to order our affairs as to maximize our joy in life.

Many of the proposals for an environmentalist ethic that are put forward nowadays are nostalgic. They want to go back to lost unities, to objective and unchanging values, and perhaps to a pre-industrial paradise. I do not think that such proposals can succeed. Instead, we need an ethic that is fully immanent or naturalistic, being based on a valuation of the here-and-now, and that recognizes that nature and culture are nowadays interwoven and in continual change. We need to see morality as an ever-renewed creative activity through which we give our life worth and keep the human enterprise going. Because this view of morality makes value entirely this-worldly, it can, I think, be called environmental; and because it emphasizes the struggle to revalue the devalued, it can, I believe, call itself Christian.

10

Nature and Culture

WHEN THEY WERE PLANNING THIS CENTENARY SERIES of Gifford Lectures, the Senatus of the University of Glasgow decided that the course was to be concerned with "various aspects of the environment—physical, spiritual, and social." In my contribution, I want to draw out some of the implications of this characteristically modern conception of the environment. I shall suggest that its emergence is part of a wider philosophical shift.

In my childhood, the environment as we now speak of it was not much in evidence. There was indeed Nature, a Greek rather than a biblical notion, which had in very varied guises been around since Aristotle; and there was also Man's Place in Nature, an important Victorian topic. But there was no environment in quite today's sense, and the word itself was not very often heard. However, I was familiar with two usages that were to contribute to our present concept.

The first was the phrase, "the environs of London," an idiom that went back as far as the seventeenth century. I had an atlas with maps of the environs of the major European cities, the point being that as towns grew rapidly in size during the later seventeenth century, people began to notice the way they sucked in workers and goods from the surrounding regions. The environs of a city were not just its geographical neighborhood or landscape setting. A complex economic relationship was involved. The environs of a city were its economic hinterland; in pre-industrial times, typically the radius from which the city was fed and populated, and in industrial times, typically the region from which people commuted daily to work in the city.

The point to remember is that when we speak of the environs of a city, of Greater London, the outer suburbs, the London region, and so forth, we are viewing the city as being not isolated but immersed in and dependent upon a living web of local traffic and economic relations with the whole region in which it is set. Indeed, one could say that a city just *is* a local concentration of various sorts of traffic and economic activity.

The second usage with which I was familiar derived from the late nineteenth century. Darwin himself did not, so far as I know, speak of the environment, but Herbert Spencer did. From the 1870s, it was customary to talk of the ways in which an organism must continually adapt itself to its environment in order to survive. This was a new and technically biological use of the term, and great stress was commonly laid on the power of the environment over the organism. The creature's environment was usually specific to it. By that I mean that the environment was not the totality of physical nature, the same for every species, but rather that for each species, its environment was merely that selection from all the ambient physical conditions that was of direct and quasi-economic relevance to its own survival-to-reproduce. In that sense, each organism had its own specific environment. But this did not imply any mitigation of the harsh pressure of the environment upon the organism. On the contrary, that pressure was often strongly emphasized. In the protracted debates about heredity and environment, an "environmentalist" was one who would today be called an environmental determinist, as distinct from a genetic determinist. That is, until the late 1950s an environmentalist was a person who stressed the primary causal influence of the environment in shaping all details of the structure and mode of existence of the organism—including the human organism. Zola and Hardy are examples of novelists who reflect this view of nature as an implacable power.

Thus in the period which I am describing—around 1875–1950—an environmentalist was a hard-nosed materialist and a kind of determinist. The environment was almost a physical God. It was a set of material conditions external to me which pressed demandingly upon me and dictated the terms on which I must live. It held the power of life and death over me, and I must adapt myself to it or perish. It was something utterly immoveable, physical necessity itself, not to be gainsaid.

In the *Supplement* to the *OED*, Volume 1 of 1972, P. S. Sears in 1956 is the earliest authority cited for the use of the word "environment" in the modern sense. In the first place, the term is no longer technically biological, but has become colloquial and almost political. Secondly, the environment is no longer sovereign physical necessity before which we all must bow, but rather is our environs. We are in a thoroughly dialectical economic relationship with it. It is all-that-out-there that both sustains our life and also has to suffer the distorting impact of our human activities upon it. Thirdly, therefore, the environment is suddenly seen to have lost its old ineluctable coercive power and to have become a fragile and vulnerable web of relationships and activities in which we are set. We have got to look after it. It needs taking care of. So, evidently, a new awareness of the power of technology, of the priority and superiority of culture over nature, and of our responsibility for maintaining the physical conditions of our own life has suddenly arrived. As a result, the concept of the environment becomes much more salient, and changes somewhat. It is as if all nature has become part of culture. The God who lorded it over us has come to be seen instead as something more like the bread and the water of our life. From then on, the rapidity with which, in Britain as in other countries, the modern range of uses of the term develops is highly remarkable: environmental safety is reported in 1957, and environmental areas in 1962. In 1967, we hear how man has contaminated his environment, and in 1970, of environmental health. In the same year, 1970, the final canonization arrives in the form of an environment minister.

Thus the environment, after taking on its modern sense in the 1950s, was by the end of the next decade the concern of a government minister and a whole department of state. Seldom can a concept have conquered so quickly.

The intellectual expression of this shift in the balance of power between nature and culture can be traced in the philosophy of the 1960s. Both in Anglo-Saxon philosophy of science and in French philosophy, it came during that period to be recognized that all our ideas about nature are produced within culture and have an intra-cultural history. Sense-perception, scientific experimentation and reporting, and the formation and debating of theories all happen inside history and are historically conditioned. Science is at no point privileged. It is itself just another cultural activity. Interpretation reaches all the way down, and we have no "pure" and extra-historical access to nature. We have no basis for distinguishing between nature itself and our own changing historically-produced representations of nature. We represent nature in a vocabulary borrowed, necessarily, from society. So the history of science is the true history of nature itself. Nature and culture have thus become thoroughly interwoven and we comprehend that we are now fully responsible, in every sense, for nature— which is what the new environmentalism is insisting. We made nature and it just *is* our descriptions of it and the way we treat it. Nature is a cultural product.

By this rather provocative remark I mean only that since we are always inside history and culture and language, and have no absolute or pure access to nature, we have no basis for separating the way the world really is from our ways of representing it. So that we do not make fetishes of our current theories, it is a good thing to keep reminding ourselves that what at any particular time is called nature is just the prevailing cultural construction of nature. Scientific knowledge needs to be "historicized."

Since 1970, the development of the concept of the environment has continued. It becomes steadily more holistic. Where the nineteenth-century environment had consisted just of physics and chemistry, the increasing interest in ecology has nowadays woven together geology, geography, and the biosphere into a single tapestry. In the 1970s, Environmental Science appeared as an academic subject. Planners started to speak of the built environment, and the city soon became as environmental as the countryside. But the most striking development of all has been the extension of the environment to include the ideal or superstructural realm. In the 1972 *Sup-*

plement to the *OED*, there is a citation from 1928 contrasting the environmental with the spiritual, the older presumption being that the environment was exclusively material or physical. Yet the Senatus in 1986 speaks of *spiritual and social aspects of the environment,* an idiom that calls for comment.

As everyone is aware, since the Second World War there has been a worldwide rediscovery and reaffirmation of the constitutive importance to the individual of mother tongue, ethnic roots, and cultural and religious identity. This complex of language, nationality, religion, and culture—for which we have no single name—has become a god to people. If they feel it is threatened, they will die for it without hesitation. Its defense has become the single most important political motive. No doubt the reason for this is that while decolonization has encouraged peoples to reassert their traditional ethnic identities, the continuing triumphant advance of Western scientific-industrial culture is at the same time effacing all local cultures. People are simultaneously and by the same historical forces being reminded and robbed of their cultural heritage. It is not surprising that they should dread the new anonymity that looms ahead of them, and should start to fight for their linguistic, cultural, and religious identity. They evidently feel that it is as necessary to their life as air and water. Since the great period in French thought of the late 1950s and 1960s, it has come to be widely accepted that we all live in a world of signs, a world, that is, of cultural meanings, beliefs, and values. These signs are not only the milieu in which we swim and the medium by which we communicate; they also, even more than the air and the water, *pass right through us,* constituting us and sustaining our life.

I have to dwell on this point, because so many Anglo-Saxons still believe in non-linguistic thought. Yet there can be no doubt that they are wrong. The public world of signs, the river of publicly-established meanings, flows straight through your head from ear to ear without a break. All your inner world is made of public materials, because you are a cultural product. That is why it is said that your language and culture give you your *identity.* There is no inner citadel where the public lan-

guage stops and pure private extra-linguistic and extra-historical thought takes over. There is no sense in the supposition
that Adam, the first man, could have been a complete and
perfect thinking and functioning human being all on his own
before Eve, before language, and before culture. On the popular traditional reading of Genesis, Adam suddenly decided one
day that it would be a good thing for him to invent language
by naming the beasts. But a moment's thought will show the
absurdity of our trying to represent to ourselves a pre-linguis-
tic being's thought that it would be a good thing if he were to
invent language. And this consideration shows us that language in a broad sense—that is, the world of signs; that is,
culture—is environmental in the strongest sense, for it is the
milieu in which we are wholly immersed, in which all our life
is lived and in which we and all other things are constituted.
As I earlier hinted that a city may be seen not as a substance
but simply as a local concentration of regional economic activity, so we may view the self not as a substance but as a communications center.

If during the past 30 years we have come progressively to
realize how important our concept of the environment is to us,
then nothing is more environmental than culture. I need my
culture as I need the air that I breathe: no wonder I'm ready
to fight for it. And, furthermore, any reasons there may be
for attempting to preserve a threatened biological species are
probably going *a fortiori* to be reasons for attempting to preserve threatened natural languages and cultures, including
ones other than our own. Looking back, I see I raised the
question of whether we should strive to preserve threatened
cultures in a little book published in 1976. I took the view
that whereas animal species are fairly easy to preserve, tribal
cultures are impossible to save because the very measures you
take to preserve them must have the effect of destroying
them. However sensitively the growth of tourism is controlled, it must destroy the local culture; and by the same
token, however protective, unobtrusive, and gently paternalis-
tic the stronger culture is in its dealings with a weaker culture,
just by being there it will destroy it. A culture cannot be quar-

antined or preserved artificially. It has to be free in its world. Put it in a zoo and it dies. A neat and fascinating paradox that brings out the way in which during our own lifetime the ancient distinction between culture and nature his been deconstructed is this: a culture can survive only in the wild state. Open it up to tourism, *or refuse to do so* and fence it off—and it dies. At home we once tried keeping a species of lizard that turned out to be unsuited to captivity. It was too tense and wild, and we couldn't tame it. I picked the poor creature up and it died of a heart attack in my hand. A culture is like that; it is a wild thing. It cannot be tamed or incorporated into anything else, which is why people around the world are so fanatically determined to fight and to die for the independence and self-respect of their ethnic group. Thus, to our earlier suggestion that nature can nowadays be seen to be a cultural product, we can add the rider that at the same time culture is, of course, a natural product.

Nothing then is more environmental than culture, and the recent incorporation of everything cultural into our concept of the environment is a most significant development. It is taken furthest by the human geographers, among whom expressions such as cultural ecology, cultural hearth, culture area, cultural landscape, and cultural geography have in recent years become well established. Here is yet one more piece of evidence that in our lifetime culture and nature, the tame and the wild, which for millennia in all societies were carefully and sharply contrasted, have now become confused and impossible any longer to distinguish from each other.

I have a hypothesis to offer about the meaning of this great event. I think the world I was born into was still in a broad sense platonic and Cartesian, but that in the last generation or so—that is to say, since about 1959—it has become thoroughly Hegelian. To explain this I shall begin from a brief but very illuminating comment in the *Dictionary of Human Geography* (1986 ed., s.v. "environmentalism") that expressly contrasts environmentalism with existentialism. The hint we are given here is that the philosophy of Sartre was very influential in the first decade after the War, but that in the late 1950s, environmentalism appeared as a sharp reaction against it.

Let us amplify that hint. In the world I was born into (and have taken so long to get out of) the essence of the human lay in consciousness and in a certain possibility of distancing oneself inwardly from nature. A very long tradition in Western thought, deriving proximately from the 'I'-philosophies of Sartre, Husserl, and Descartes, and ultimately from Augustine and Plato, defined the human in terms of individual spiritual subjectivity. As human, I knew myself to be a unique, immortal, rational soul. What defined me as human was my inward stepping-back into subjectivity and away from the common natural world, together with my immateriality and my capacity for God. God himself was pure, deified, absolute subjectivity, and it was in the relation to God, and *only* in that relation, that my personal identity could be perfected. To constitute and perfect me, I didn't need the world, nor the body, nor the passions, nor even other people. I needed only God. So I did not actually *have* to have any environment at all, as Descartes makes so clear. The self-before-God can stand quite alone. Its identity is constituted metaphysically and not socially.

As late as Husserl and Sartre—that is, until the early 1950s—this very ancient spiritual individualism lingered, albeit latterly in a secularized form. Put crudely and strongly, its three principal doctrines are that the self is a substance, that the self is spiritual or immaterial, and that the self's relations with its physical environment are merely external to it, contingent, and not constitutive of it. Consciousness is seen as the primary philosophical certainty, and the conscious self, observing and deliberating, stands back a little from the world. It is a little sub-world on its own. It is not unaffected by natural events; on the contrary, it registers them all the time. But it is not *constituted* by what it does and what happens to it, so that the familiar jibe, "the ghost in the machine" is fair enough as an epitome of how the mind-body relation is seen. Although the early Sartre himself was anti-Freudian, it was perfectly possible for the mind-body dualist to allow that we also have a "lower nature" of animal origin, which is indeed bound into the world. But when the Christian related herself to God in prayer, when the scientist observed, experimented, and reasoned, and when the moral agent resolved, legislated, and posited values, *then* you transcended both nature and your own lower nature to become your real self. Once again, the real self is the self *that becomes itself as it distances itself* from the world, the body, and the passions. As certain visitors were speedily sent down to the servants' quarters, so Darwin and Freud could be received, provided that they were promptly referred only to our lower nature. They were to be used ascetically. Yes, they had disclosed something of our lower nature. All the more reason for keeping it firmly in its place. So Darwin and Freud could be employed to reinforce rather than to undermine the traditional supernaturalism of the rational self. Their subject-matter was precisely that in us which the supernatural self conquered, escaped, and transcended as it drew away from nature.

Against this background we begin to see why environmentalism has been expressly contrasted with existentialism by some writers. When I was in my teens, around 1950, the leading cultural influences of the day were Sartre's existentialism, a rather aggressive scientism, and popular neo-orthodox Christianity. I was influenced strongly by all three, even though at the time they seemed very different from each other. Now they look like triplets. They were all in a broad sense platonic. They all taught the metaphysics of spiritual individualism. The value-gaining movement in the spiritual life was the one whereby the self recollects itself, steps back from its too-easy immersion in the passions and the flux of life, distances itself from its own lower nature, and becomes spiritual, disengaged, purely rational, and free. It thus takes up the correct stance for conquering the world by gaining objective knowledge, by moral legislation, by purity of heart, and by relating itself to God. The age was still broadly Cartesian, and I was a follower of science and Augustinian Christianity, of Kant and Kierkegaard.

I hinted earlier that I regard the environmental movement as part of a large-scale cultural shift that has taken us in a more

Hegelian direction. We now see why. Environmental thinking
works against the spiritual-substance theory of the self. In fact
we all of us, I believe, now detest the way in which that view
of the self systematically disparaged our supposedly "lower"
nature, the body, the passions, and our social and physical environs. We now find somewhat egoistic and unappealing the
idea of becoming more real by stepping back into privacy and
subjectivity. We do not want to spend all our lives wishing
that we were in a better world, somewhere else. Increasingly
nowadays we incline to a social, a historical, and an external-
relations view of the self. I am not a spiritual substance from
another world that is merely contingently related to its life in
the here and now. My life is not the life of an outsider who
finds himself temporarily trapped and reluctantly acting a part
in this world. I just am my own life. I am not a substance: I
simply am the aggregate of all the myriad small events, trans-
actions, economic exchanges, and symbolic communications
that comprise my life. What you see and hear is all there is. I
am only skin deep. I am quite *happy* to be only skin deep. The
real me is all on my own skin surface, where culture meets
nature. Beneath the surface there is only biology. The traditional metaphysics of substance was thoroughly alienating in
the strict sense that it taught us to think of ourselves as being
aliens, extra-terrestrials, or indeed spies, because your true
identity was not your publicly-manifest identity but a second,
secret identity known only to you and to your divine Control.
Oh yes, *spy-fiction is theological,* and this particular theological
metaphysics of a hidden inner self had originated early in the
Iron Age as a consciousness-raising device. It was associated
with a dualism of world-above and world-below, soul and
body, reason and the passions, the necessary and the contingent, and so on, with a characteristic set of religious beliefs
and ascetical practices. It did a great job in its day, but it's
dead now. We need a different metaphysics, immanent and
transactional. It will enable me to say that I am not an alien
but just my life, the sum of all the events involving me, and
woven into my environment like any other organism by myri-

ads of small daily dealings, much as the city is woven into its
environs.

Thus environmental thinking has an affinity with the work
of the semiologists, the structuralists, and others who look to
Durkheim, to Saussure, and, above all, to Hegel. With one
voice they all say that the individual does not stand alone. We
are always already within language and culture and history,
embodied (or rather, embedded) with others in a world. No
particular piece of behavior can be intelligible, no utterance
can make sense, and I can't even think a thought intelligible
to myself, without that great public matrix and thesaurus
being already presupposed and in place. Human life is essentially lived in a medium of which we are part, which sustains
us and which continually flows right through us. From the scientific point of view, this medium may be called nature, or the
environment, and seen as consisting in a great flowing swarm
of minute events. From the philosophical point of view, the
medium may be seen as a semantic field or as a "Sea of Meanings," that is, a vast shifting expanse of differentiated and
scaled feelings, valuations, and meanings. So the whole environment in which we live and move and have our being is on
the one face of it Culture and on the other Nature; on one
side Thought and on the other Being; on one side Language
and on the other side the World. In relation to this unbounded
whole our self-conscious individuality is not primary, as Descartes and Husserl claimed, but merely secondary.

I suggested at the beginning that the emergence of our
modern concept of the environment was a sign of and a part
of a larger philosophical shift from Plato to Hegel, from certain
traditional styles of dualism and foundationalism to a new vision of the world as a boundless immanently-evolving whole
in which we are fully immersed and which has no outside. I
no longer see myself as in any way *protruding* from my world.
In the older way of thinking there was a supernatural world
above, there was an ideal order of timeless standards governing our thought and conduct, and both God and the self were
spiritual substances, the one being Infinite and the other his
finite counterpart. These metaphysical beliefs were somewhat

double-edged. On the one hand, it has to be said in their favor that they did hold the life-world firmly in place, anchoring it to eternity rather as the space inside a great marquee is held open by guy-lines, invisible to the crowd inside the tent, that run down to tent-pegs outside. Even people who never go to church like to see churches in the landscape because for them, too, an ancient church is a site away from which a guy-line runs invisibly out to eternity and holds this world steady. So the old metaphysical beliefs reassuringly and comfortingly anchored the world to a point outside it. They gave us security and they held the world upright, but, on the other hand, a price had to be paid for these comforts. The contingent natural world in which our life is set was relatively devalued. Life's center of gravity was shifted out of life altogether. Nature became the Other, ambiguous, female, subordinate, threatening, tempting, moody, changeable, and we drew back nervously from her, fearing that she might swallow us up. Thus a good deal of the patriarchal metaphysics and symbolism of Christianity and of platonism was designed to encourage us to develop an autonomous masculine rational ego, consciously independent and self-distanced from our Mother/Matrix. To become spiritual, free, and adult you had to become a substance, and to become a substance you had to pull away from Mother Nature. That is, you had to be anti-environmental.

The curious feature of the times we live in is that all these ideas are in the melting pot at once—the founding doctrines of Western philosophy and religion, the relation of culture to nature, the cultural construction of gender, and all our ideas about spiritual freedom, power, and authority. We dimly see that these themes are connected, and we dimly see that environmentalism, linked as it is with feminism, the peace movement, and so forth, has called them all into question simultaneously. We are aware that a period of revolutionary change has begun, but we do not so clearly see where it may take us. Some people are apocalyptically pessimistic about the end of Western thought, and almost everyone thinks that Christianity is invested to the hilt in the old realistic metaphysics and cannot survive its downfall.

I disagree. In classical Christian thought the soul was oddly divided by being tugged in two different directions. One path to salvation was that of the monk: we were supposed to turn away from this world and to look only to the heavenly world above for solid joys and lasting treasures. The other path was that of St. Francis: it led you sideways to your fellow-creatures and to everything that is merely contingent and lowly. Under the old dispensation the two paths were never fully synthesized. They could not be synthesized while the motives that had originally distanced God from the world, the self from the world, and the self from God remained active. Hegel's philosophy of mediation and reconciliation points to the coming of an age when the old dualisms and disjunctions, once thought essential to culture, are to be overcome by a compensatory movement of healing and synthesis. In this development, he saw Christianity's fulfillment, not its abolition; and I have suggested that we should see environmentalism in the same way. There is a whole cluster of contemporary movements that are variously Green, pacific, feminist, vegetarian, small-scale, quasi-Buddhist, and so forth, and that see our inherited cultural structures as having been excessively dualistic, repressive, and antagonistic. Perhaps a new culture is trying to come to birth, and perhaps that new culture may one day come to be seen as renewing rather than replacing Christianity.

Let me conclude by suggesting how this might be so. Human thinking is and always was binary. It proceeds by separating this from that, the right hand from the left, and the above from the below. Wherever a line was drawn, a preference was expressed. Thus culture made a house for us to live in, an ordered and hierarchized vision of the world that was sacralized, sealed, and protected by religion. Yet while it is seemingly necessary to human life that the world shall be thus divided up, ranked, and ordered, we appear to find it painful that our experience should be polarized in this way. I ask myself why, in order to be able to be myself and to think myself, I have got to be estranged from God, estranged from woman, and estranged from wild nature. So I find myself looking also to religion for reconciliation and the restoration of unity. But this means that religion ends up oddly two-faced. On the one hand it intransigently defends cultural distinctions, while on the other hand, its rituals and myths simultaneously offer a tantalizing promise that the same disjunctions can be healed and overcome.

Now although philosophy ostensibly began as a protest against and an alternative to traditional ways of thinking, it in fact merely continued them by other means. Philosophy's chief problem is always to define itself, and how can it do so except by declaring that it is concerned with this and not that? Thus philosophy, too, divides and prefers, making the form/matter distinction in order to choose for itself the world of form, the reason/passions distinction in order to express its preference for the world of reason, and so on. In the most typically philosophical philosophers, Plato and Kant, it looks as if philosophical reflection just works by generating ever more variations on basically the same type of distinction. One can become weary of this obsessive elaboration, and Hegel sought out what he called "speculative germs" in the Kantian system, hints as to how it might be possible to reverse the movement and join the world up again.

Historic Christianity was a fusion of religion and platonism, so that it conspicuously exhibits all the traits that I am describing. In it, the creation theme pictures God as standing over against us, laying down all the distinctions and establishing a structured and hierarchized cosmos for us to inhabit. By contrast, the redemption theme reversed and undoes all this, reconciling all the polarized oppositions and antagonisms and returning into us everything that formerly stood over against us—including God, who is distributed as spirit so that he becomes one in many and we become many in one.

The patterns of thinking I have been trying to unfold have shown, I hope, that the popular association of the environmental movement with the Christian doctrine of creation is a complete mistake. The doctrine of creation that developed out of Genesis was concerned to define a power-structure. The chain of command ran: God, his angels, the heavenly bodies, human souls, men's bodies, women's bodies, the beasts, plants, and so on. By contrast, environmental thinking is part of a widespread reaction against the metaphysics of substance, hierarchy, power, and control. It criticizes the historic doctrine of man's lordship over nature as God's viceroy, and counter-attacks with its own strange new notions of animal rights, speciesism, and the like. In short, as Hegel's thought makes clear, the true affinity of the environmental movement is with the Christian doctrine of redemption, and *not* the doctrine of creation.

The redemption theme has not yet become properly developed in Christianity, but it is best seen as an attempt to separate value from power. Orthodox Christianity so far has been a religion of power. That which was higher in value lorded it over that which was lower. Every value-difference was a difference of rank and every rank-difference was a difference of power. But however subdued it was, there could always be heard, far-off and faintly, the theme of redemption. People dreamt of the possibility that God himself might cease to lord it over us, by returning into us and so no longer being objectively over against us. When that happened there would no longer be any justification for the domination of inferiors by superiors. The soul need not buffet the body, men would no longer rule over women, and human beings generally would stop exploiting the beasts and the earth. It would then become obvious that our cosmologies and the metaphysics of substance had been mere tools of power. They could be forgotten.

In this way, then, the environmental movement invites us to become critically aware of the cosmic politics that has hitherto inspired both our technology and our religion. If we can get there, the new awareness may do us and our religion a lot of good.

BIBLIOGRAPHY

Aristotle. *Metaphysics.* D iv. "Nature." In *Aristotle's Metaphysics.* G, D, E, translated by J. D. Kirwan, with Notes. Oxford University Press, 1971, pp. 32–34.

Cupitt, Don. *Life Lines*. SCM Press, 1986.

————. *The Long Legged Fly*. SCM Press, 1987.

————. *The New Christian Ethics*. SCM Press, 1988.

Derrida, Jacques. *Speech and Phenomena*. Northwestern University Press, 1973.

————. *Margins of Philosophy*. Harvester Press, 1982.

Douglas, Mary. *Natural Symbols*. Barrie & Rockliffe, 1970.

Foucault, Michel. *The Order of Things*. Tavistock Publications, 1970.

Harland, Michel. *Superstructuralism: the Philosophy of Structuralism and Post-Structuralism*. Methuen, 1987.

Huxley, T. H. *Man's Place in Nature and other Essays*. J. M. Dent, 1906.

Johnson, R. J., et al., eds. *The Dictionary of Human Geography*. 2nd ed. s.vv. "Environmentalism," "environmental determinism," "culture," "cultural ecology," etc. Basil Blackwell, 1986.

Kuhn, T. S. *The Structure of Scientific Revolutions*. University of Chicago Press, 1962.

Lacan, Jacques. *Écrits: A Selection*. Tavistock Publications, 1977.

Parfit, Derek. *Reasons and Persons*. Oxford University Press, 1984.

Sarup, Madam. *An Introductory Guide to Post-Structuralism and Postmodernism*. Harvester Wheatsheaf, 1988.

Soper, Kate. *Humanism and Anti-Humanism*. Hutchinson, 1986.

Staten, Henry. *Wittgenstein and Derrida*. Basil Blackwell, 1985.

Taylor, Mark. *Erring: A Postmodern Anthology*. University of Chicago Press, 1984.

Thomas, Keith. *Man and the Natural World: A History of the Modern Sensibility*. Pantheon Books, 1983.

Whitehead, A. N. *The Concept of Nature*. Cambridge University Press, 1920.

5
Replying to Critics

11

A Reply to Rowan Williams

IN HIS ARTICLE "Religious Realism" Rowan Williams has discussed my books *Taking Leave of God* (1980) and *The World to Come* (1982), finding in them many things that surprise me.

A full-dress reply would be inappropriate. Once a book has grown up and left home the author can do no more for it. It may die a natural death or it may wander for years before it finds the reader to whom it can open its heart, but in neither case can it be helped. Besides, who dare claim today either that a text has just one correct interpretation or that the author is the best person to supply it? Whatever clarity of writing may be, it is an illusion to suppose that one can use it in order to coerce a reader into reading a text in just one way. What is more, the two books in question are among those of my writings that, for a religious reason, were actually composed as equivocal riddles. Jacques Derrida has a few relevant sentences that, as usual with him, go swiftly to the heart of the matter:

> Just as there is a negative theology, so there is a negative atheology. An accomplice of the former, it still pronounces the absence of a center, when it is play that should be affirmed. But is not the desire for a center, as function of play itself, the indestructible itself? And in the repetition or return of play, how could the phantom of the center not call to us?

This enjoyable, ambiguous dance between affirmation and negation—or, more precisely, between an affirmation of God which is obliged nevertheless to seek to negate itself, and a denial of God which also by its own compulsive backward glance tends constantly to negate itself and become affirmation again—has long seemed to me to encompass something of the mystery of theism. It was already prominent even before *The Leap of Reason* was written in 1973. I like the idea that a sense of the presence of God is curiously hard to distinguish from a sense of the absence of God, and even more do I like the fact that the one may function in a person's life in much the same way as the other. The silence of the early Wittgenstein, the Wittgenstein of the *Tractatus* and of the house in Vienna, captures this ambiguity beautifully.

Yet at precisely this point I wonder whether Rowan Williams can disagree with me. He has little to say in favor of theological realism of the type that I have criticized, and produces no classical-type metaphysical arguments in support of it. Instead he speaks of *religious* realism. On the evidence of his published writings, all this means is that he is a religious symbolist who takes his symbols seriously. A doctrinal rather than a philosophical theologian, he clings to realism in order to postpone having to face the crisis with which my books deal, namely the end of theological realism. But as Karl Barth's writings long ago made clear, religious realism without old-style metaphysical underpinning remains within the sphere of what Derrida calls "play." And Rowan Williams himself effectively concedes this by deciding to discuss my books at the level of spirituality; that is, by setting aside questions of dogmatic metaphysics and talking as I do in terms of the way our religious ideas work out in our lives.

Rowan Williams is, of course, correct in setting aside attempts to provide the old pre-critical type of metaphysical underpinning for realism. It is too hopelessly discredited by now, too incorrigibly vague and self-deceiving to do the job required of it; which is just as well, because if it were to succeed it would destroy faith in any case. For an objective realist God is precisely *not* the God of religion, who is *essentially* a my-god, bound to the believer whose god he is. And I think that Rowan Williams probably realizes this. So how do we differ? By my many express statements, as well by the fact that we both practice the same faith and recite the same Liturgy, it is clear that I as well as Rowan Williams affirm the value of *religious* realism—within the sphere of play. And he, as well as I, acknowledges that such religious realism (linguistic, attitudinal, and so forth) needs to be qualified by irony, and is subject to built-in checks and balances—that also operate within the sphere of play. So it appears that there is no significant difference between us, and I am left wondering why he should need to begin his article by saying that the books under discussion are unpopular, "represent a challenge," and so forth. On whose behalf is he taking up the cudgels, and why? I shall try to demonstrate that his vestigial and groundless attachment to realism puts him on the side of Christendom against Christianity, and I shall urge him to change sides.

It should be said at the outset that the two texts in question are very different in their intellectual standpoint. *Taking Leave of God* is strongly Kantian, and reflects the influences of Mansel's theory that religious truth is regulative, and of Wittgenstein's interpretation of Kierkegaard. In retrospect, I now see it as completing a development that began as far back as *Christ and the Hiddenness of God* (1971), and even earlier. *The World to Come*, by contrast, reflects the recent joining of hands between American and French philosophy as seen, for example, in what Rorty has lately been writing about Derrida. Standing within the post-Nietzschean tradition, it represents a new departure. Thus (if the author's view of the matter is worth anything) *Taking Leave of God* rounded off what I had been trying to say for the previous dozen years, and it was followed rather than preceded by the conversion that led me to write the second book.

However, alongside these intellectual differences there is also a strong resemblance between the two books. They were both designed not as works of spirituality but rather as spiritual exercises; not only indirect communications but also "existence-communications," in Kierkegaard's phrase. They were supposed to be tools for bringing about religious change in the reader, and are thus themselves examples of that instrumentalism that Rowan Williams rather mysteriously deplores (and it is only because they have so signally failed to work that I am going as far as this toward "explaining" them). *Taking Leave of God* was a brisk forced march along the negative way intended to be a purge for our engrained eudaemonism and thereby also to purify the concept of religion (a subject which had much occupied me in earlier books). *The World to Come* was intended to be a more specifically and purely Christian work. Encountering modern nihilism, and experiencing it as Holy Saturday and the end of the world, it enacts the pattern of death and resurrection. It seeks to lead its reader to die with Christ, to experience the Nihil, and to come to such a pass that he sees that there is no other recourse left him but to choose the values of the Kingdom of God on the far side.

Naturally, the underlying question is this: in the Nihil, why choose the values of Christ rather than those of Schopenhauer, or Nietzsche, or Sartre, for example? That is a very interesting question. An answer is attempted in the book, but at the time of writing I did not yet realize how much help is given on this point by Albert Schweitzer, for I did not know how seriously Schweitzer had wrestled with Nietzsche around the year 1900. I shall correct the injustice to Schweitzer in another place.

To resume: within *The World to Come*, various literary tricks are used. Some readers may have noticed them in chapter 3, for example, where they were set close to the surface: note the different literary levels of the three sections, and the ironical title. The point about the chapter title is that I was taken aback by the public reaction to *Taking Leave of God*, so I was here signaling that the second book was so strongly Christian that there was no likelihood of its being understood. And so it has turned out; for *The World to Come* was indeed an absurdly ambitious attempt to Christianize modern nihilism by incorporating it into, and making of it an episode within, the classic mythic dramas of death and rebirth, the end of the world and the coming of the Kingdom of God. Nietzsche had taken these dramas and dechristianized them: I was attempting to wrest them back from him.

It is because of all this that I see faith not as a privileged way of gaining reassuring supernatural information—as, in short, a superstition—but as an ultimate and creative choice made in a moment of darkness in which all such spurious consolations have been irretrievably lost.

Both books are therefore voluntaristic, its doctrine of the

will and of the radical freedom of faith being not (as Rowan
Williams thinks) Luciferean or Promethean, but Christianity's
glory. For years I had been attracted and repelled by Christ's
preaching of the end of the world. If the secret of Christianity
can somehow only be unlocked by experiencing within oneself that event, then clearly we must reach a point at which
there is no longer any possibility of appeal to nature or to the
emotions, nor any question of grounding our values in the way
the world is. We have to reach a point where nothing remains
except a pure creative choice *ex nihilo* (i.e., precisely to get
ourselves out of the Nihil), and that choice—provided we
really do make it in the right place—is faith. Cosmological
religion, allied as it is with metaphysics and worldly power, is
at an end.

And that is why I suggested that Rowan Williams's residual
(and by now groundless) attachment to cosmological religion
and to realism has put him on the side of Christendom against
Christianity. For he is saying that it is, after all, not necessary
to die with Christ and to pass through the Nihil, that fearsome
moment in which one loses everything, even knowledge and
society. Christendom protects us from all that, for it allows us
to take our faith and our values from the way the world is and
the powers that be. Christendom sees Christ's gospel of dying
to the world, with its corollaries of nihilism and radical freedom, as anarchic and subversive. It is a "Prometheanism of
the will," a presumptuous attempt to create new values
(namely, values other than those of Christendom), too hard
for ordinary people, too unpopular, too individualistic.

The hands may be those of Rowan Williams, but the voice
is the voice of Ivan Karamazov's Grand Inquisitor—though in
justice it must be said that the Grand Inquisitor would never
have risked overplaying his hand by hinting that the burden
of freedom Christ lays upon us is somehow linked with *capi-
talism*. That is a giveaway, for it betrays too openly the influence of the great catholomarxist consensus, which for the
people's sake and in their name will always reject Christ's
freedom in favor of security.

Teasing?—but there is a great issue at stake here, and it has to be pursued. A few years ago our leading church newspaper published an Ascension Day editorial that declared that the Ascension of Christ gave the lie to the modern humanism that would set man on the throne of the Universe. It was a hilarious example of the way in which in certain church quarters, an instinctive sadism, a will to put human beings down, is *always* more constant and reliable than any grasp of the Christian gospel. For what on earth or in heaven is Christ's Ascension if he is not the first of many brethren, and if we are not to ascend whither he has gone before? More generally, what is the point of any religious representation if we are forbidden to regard it as an ideal that we may hope to attain? Why *worship* what one may not aspire after?

I raise this question in the light of Rowan Williams's citation of a sentence from *Taking Leave of God:* "The work of religion is to celebrate the triumph of universal, free and sovereign consciousness, emancipated from and lord over nature." My language here is clearly borrowed from the enthronement psalms of antiquity, in which worshippers celebrated the sovereignty of the creator-god over the natural order. In Christianity this language is transferred to the exalted and glorified *man* Jesus, as we are reminded by the Propers of the Ascension. Believers, worshipping the exalted Jesus, express their faith and hope that what he is they will themselves become—and even, in an anticipatory sense, already are. Christ is exalted, not to dominate them gentile-style, but rather to prepare a place for his followers, to become the first of many brethren.

Thus although Christendom may indeed be a project for restoring religious heteronomy, Christianity is quite certainly a project for overcoming it. I briefly reminded readers of the fact that Hegel and his young followers saw this point very clearly by giving a slight Hegelian flavor to the wording of the sentence; but anyone who prefers a more "orthodox" authority can find in John Keble's hymn for Whitsunday in *The Christian Year* (as stodgily orthodox a source as I can think of) an admirable summary of the themes of *Taking Leave of God*.

The sentence was, then, so worded that I could move into

position behind it a whole complex history: the Old Testament, its fulfillment and hominization in Christ, and the
young-Hegelian understanding of Christianity's inner meaning, as developed in one way by Feuerbach and in another by
Kierkegaard. I could spend a great deal of time on further
analysis, for example, of the choice of the word "work," and
of the way the sentence evokes simultaneously the attributes
of God, the way God functions as the religious ideal, and the
believer's aspiration to participate in the divine attributes; but
I must not bore the reader. It is sufficient simply to ask why
Rowan Williams should overlook what the detailed construction and wording of the sentence says, italicize the words *triumph, sovereign, emancipated* and *lord*—and then censure the
conception of faith that they imply.

This is most surprising, because the ideas in question are
highly scriptural and figure largely in our daily devotions. Why
are they being attacked? Can it be that Rowan Williams, although, as he tells us, a professional, has been so swept away
by the general belief that Cupitt is Promethean (or something
of the kind) that he fails to notice that he is attacking the very
heart of the Christian hope of redemption? Is not this a case
where Christendom's will to punish presumption and put
down human pride has triumphed over Christianity's optimism about the possibility of human liberation?

Why does this happen? Both *Taking Leave of God* and *The
World to Come* were much concerned with the problem and
with producing a theory to account for it. Briefly, the realist
religious psychology ceased to be a live option, for the ablest
people, after the time of Kant and Hegel. In Britain, always a
little behindhand, the generation that grew up with Newman
in the 1820s were in their psychology still confident realists,
whereas those who grew up in the 1840s were no longer so.
But the churches, battling with darwinism, biblical criticism,
and the rest, remained psychologically attached to realism
even though they could not (and still cannot) give a satisfactory account of what it *means*. From then on the maintenance
of realist faith in the individual required a small inner falsity,
an occlusion of consciousness, which meant that *the believer*

was no longer aware of the true character of his own act of believing.
He had become like a cultist.

This development has, in the long term, had disastrous effects. It has produced the strange but all-pervasive modern inner alienation of Christians from the true meaning of their own faith. It made faith vulnerable to reductive psychological analysis by Freud and others. Ordinary people, highly sensitive in these matters, detect the inner repression and resistance to consciousness by which the realist religious psychology is maintained, and draw their own conclusions. They note how within the minds of theologians, and between the theologians and the churches, there is a prolonged struggle between myth and criticism, enchantment and consciousness.

So the problem of *aggiornamento* is essentially a problem of healing our divided religious psychology and making a truly modern faith fully aware of itself, without the repression, fear, and punitiveness that are still so depressingly familiar to us all. Hence the emphasis on consciousness in the two books: I am simply saying that it is necessary that believers should not deceive themselves, but should know and understand clearly what their own believing is.

At this point Rowan Williams charges me with "cultural determinism," and I concede that in *Taking Leave of God* I did subscribe to the Hegelian belief, still of course prominent in Freud and Jung, that consciousness does and should grow and progress. But in the second book, under the impact of the Nietzschean critique of it, that belief disappears and I now confine myself to saying that mentalities change. To be sane, rational and effective faith needs to express itself in terms of the prevailing mentality; although it is very important to insist that this does *not* mean that it should allow itself to be assimilated to contemporary values. Liberal theology accommodates itself to the contemporary mentality *and* its values, and so loses the distinctively Christian categories. Radical theology has a different strategy. It learns the local language, it learns to express itself in terms intelligible to the prevailing mentality, precisely in order most effectively to *challenge* the age with the Christian categories and values.

The radical strategy is the only one that can preserve the Christian categories. Liberalism leads to dissolution; and a nostalgic Christendom-type religion, deprived of the social and cultural context in which it was intelligible, dwindles into an ineffectual closed circle of cognitive deviants. There are those who look to the East with admiration, and would like the Western churches to go the way of the Orthodox churches, but I am not among them.

So I appeal to Rowan Williams to consider changing sides. I cannot offer much in the way of inducements, for to do so it is necessary to pass through the worst thing in the world, the Nihil. But there is one consolation. The blessed sign that one has indeed managed to negotiate that fearful crossing is still given: they throw you out of the synagogues.

12

A Reply to David Edwards

The Vision of Christ that thou dost see
Is my Vision's Greatest Enemy . . .

WILLIAM BLAKE

THE NON-REALIST INTERPRETATION of religious language that
has become very widespread around the world in recent years
is not a pure innovation. Among the precursors of it that I have
elsewhere cited are fideism, biblical and Protestant voluntarism, and, especially, the long tradition of the Negative Way
in theology. To keep the gods describable, the ancient Greeks
had always kept them finite. When, after Plotinus (third century A.D.), the God of mainline Christian Platonic theology
finally transcended the categories altogether and became infinite, he thereby became officially ineffable and incomprehensible. So our religious language ceased to be able
confidently to latch on to an Object external to it—and the
seeds of modern non-realism were sown. Non-realism is not
an aberration, but has grown directly out of the highest of
high orthodoxy (which, as David Edwards will know, is what
happened in my own well-documented case).

A further impetus to the emergence of theological non-realism was given by the two great founders of modern thought,
Kant and Hegel. Both were Lutherans, but both knew that
the age of supernatural belief had ended. For Kant, God was
an Ideal of Reason and a moral postulate: hence my phrase,
"a guiding spiritual ideal." For Hegel, God coincided with the
universal human Spirit unfolding in history toward its consummation: hence the occasional use by me and other non-
realists of the Feuerbach-Jung notion of God as the greater
Self that we are to become, and our occasional talk of God as
having in Christ and the Spirit "died" into humanity.

All major subsequent theologians have been greatly influenced by Kant or Hegel or both, so that the greater part of post-Kantian theology *can* be read in a non-realistic sense. Of course, any text is capable of various readings, and there is no such thing as the one True reading. But a text like Kierkegaard's *Purity of Heart* certainly can—as I reported back in the 1970s—be read non-realistically. God is real as one prays to him. God is internal to religious language and practice. God, exacting, transcendent, just, holy, and merciful, functions as an eternal standpoint within the religious consciousness, from which one's life is assessed, examined, and judged. It is most important to understand that a writer such as D. Z. Phillips uses all the customary language about God to just the same effect as a realist, while yet in the philosophy of religion, he is in fact a non-realist. So far as everyday religious practice and utterance are concerned, the non-realist may well be indistinguishable from the realist, and one may have to search for very small tell-tale signs to spot the difference. There may not be any, in which case the writer can be understood either way. For example, T. S. Eliot was certainly exposed to the non-realistic interpretations of religious language that are to be found in his philosophical master F. H. Bradley and in Indian mysticism, but I cannot just now recall a text where Eliot is explicit about his own view.

However, during the 1980s I have obviously done more than offer a philosophical analysis of standard idioms. I have also wanted to destabilize standard idioms, putting forward a range of philosophical arguments about the endlessness of interpretation, the social and historical relativity of all meaning, and the provisional and humanly manufactured character of truth in the modern period. From these and other considerations it follows that in our time we must see realities of every sort as established only within our ever-changing human conversation. There is no faculty in a modern university that any longer transmits fixed, objective, and given truth. In every faculty, including that of theology, truth is now a running debate. You can only report the current state of the argument. That is all there is. So we have now got to see religion in a quite new way. It is not a supernatural datum. It is an ever-renewed imaginative and productive human activity. Thus my late-1980s "post-modern" writings have come to look rather like radicalized versions of the Roman Catholic modernism of the early years of the twentieth century.

How well David Edwards understands the history of philosophy and theology, the issue between realists and non-realists, and the present state of Christian thought, I leave it to the reader to decide. But the tone of what Edwards has written points to a third level of disagreement between us. He would presumably profess himself content with the faith and the church as he first received them and as they still are, whereas I want root-and-branch reform as soon as possible. That we are in a frightful mess should have become apparent just these past few years, just in Britain. Or indeed, just these past few years, just in Rome.

The problem is partly one of the political context. Right-wing politics assigns a number of roles to the church, as an arm of the heritage industry, as a concealer of the reality of social change, as a legitimator, and as an engine for the mass-production of authoritarian personalities—all of which ought to be making us Christians very rebellious indeed. But apart from all that, the church is in any case still locked into a hopelessly inappropriate medieval world-view, a paranoid patriarchal rationality, and a psychologically repressive vocabulary, which are preposterously at variance with her claim to stand for human redemption. Until we put things right, the whole apparatus will increasingly do people more harm than good.

It is no use saying that there have been some humane and reasonable modern theologians. If there have been, they have made no difference. Look at the texts in our standard authorized prayer books and hymn books. How much has changed? Take a devotional companion such as Milner-White's *Daily Prayer* (one of the very *best*) and analyze in the manner of modern literary theory just what values are being recommended, what ethical and ontological scales are being constructed, and what world-view is being presupposed. The results, I promise, turn out to be quite horrifying to a present-day sensibility.

The chief reason for this extraordinary value-shift is that in recent years, *feminism has spread to men*. I warned nearly twenty years ago that feminism was going to present a major challenge to the church, but for a long time it seemed that the radical Christian feminist critique of the church's language and institutions was going to be ghettoized or kept out on the periphery. Now, however, the revolt is spreading to men as well. A great deal of what has come down to us now feels like sexist ideology grown old and very sick. Even a fairly old-fashioned and unreconstructed heterosexual male like me finds it unendurable. We cannot defend it. We must clean it up, for what on earth can be the point of waxing indignant in defense of a form of Christianity that no longer makes people whole?

We must change, and the sooner the better. My recent writings may seem inadequate to me and highly excessive to others, but I have at least been attempting to open some pathways of intellectual, moral, and religious renewal. And since the Church can only be changed from within, I shall stay and serve her as best I can. Fortunately, Anglican formularies nowhere say either that the Church is infallible and irreformable, or that priests have got to be metaphysical realists.

INDEX